Game Change

Transform Your Business Future

Elliot Forte
Jonathan Sharp

www.businessthink.co.uk

Acknowledgements

For over 20 years we have supported businesses in the field and we want to thank the thousands of entrepreneurs who welcomed us into their lives and trusted us with their futures. We learnt something new from every single one and Game Change is the result.

We would also like to thank all of our colleagues over the years who always cared deeply about helping businesses and were willing to share their knowledge. We would like to particularly mention Nigel Best, whose insights influenced our approach on finance; the late Rob Kinna whose work on process improvement is the inspiration for Chapter 8; and the late Denise Anderson who in her short time at the helm of Business Link for Norfolk showed us what a learning company could be.

We would also like to thank Richard Adams at Plymouth University, John Carter at Somerset Council and Steve Turner at Devon County Council who decided to commission Business Think to create the Game Change workshops as part of the EU Open Innovation Pilot. It is always difficult to secure your first funded project and we will always be grateful for being given the opportunity.

We would also like to thank the 36 entrepreneurs who attended the Game Change workshops, giving up three days of their valuable time with very little idea of what to expect in return. Their positive feedback drove us on to write this book and share that experience with other business leaders.

Finally, most of all we would like to thank our families who support us unconditionally and often pay the price for our vision, risk taking and hard work.

Elliot and Jonathan

Contents

Introduction

What are you capable of in business?

You are probably reading this book because deep down you aren't really sure.

Over the past 20 years, we have worked closely with literally thousands of entrepreneurs from all walks of life and backgrounds. Not in a superficial way, but at the heart of their business, working on strategy and, more importantly, how that impacts on their life outside work. In every single scenario, the common denominator was always the same: whether successful or not, the leader is always the main barrier to growing a business.

We want to be clear about the driving force behind this book. Although we don't know you, we believe in you because we are yet to meet a single human being in business who didn't have potential to build a great enterprise and be happy. This should be no surprise to you. You breathe the same air as everyone else, so understanding that you are no worse and no better than the greatest business people, is critical to your success. These entrepreneurs are successful for emotional reasons, not because of their DNA. They do better because they embrace focus, not process. They possess an unwavering belief in themselves, not others. They are great entrepreneurs not because they do as others say, but because they do whatever it takes.

Stop cluttering your mind with books that advocate 'business by numbers'. Stop watching programmes like The Apprentice and Dragon's Den. If that was the way to transform your business future, we all would have done it by now. Instead, start thinking for yourself and start believing in yourself. Because, contrary to popular opinion, it's inherently simple to be a great entrepreneur.

Whatever happened to simple? The truth is you can't make money by selling simple. So people sell complex instead.

Business people like Alan Sugar didn't read books to learn how to grow a business. They did it by believing in themselves and observing others. In his autobiography "What You See is What You Get" Lord Sugar explains how he learnt the art of sales as a young man by observing traders on Chelmsford market. That catalyst gave him the confidence and skills to launch Amstrad, not reading hundreds of business books. He created his own personal apprenticeship in enterprise.

You won't find complex business theory in this book. You won't find elaborate processes designed to turn you into a robot, disguised as a 'business person'. You won't find anything to justify our own existence as authors.

What you will find is simplicity. We will help you realise how brilliant you can be in business, not just today but every day. We will share with you what we have experienced and observed working with those thousands of entrepreneurs, their strengths and weaknesses. You will receive the minimum amount of structure needed to allow you to be yourself as an entrepreneur, the greatest asset you have. We will show you how to unleash the most powerful weapon in any business – you.

The Wheel of Confusion

"To make money, requires a clear brain.
No one can succeed in business unless a person has a brain to enable laying of plans, and reason to guide them in their execution, no matter how bountifully a person may be blessed with intelligence."

P.T. Barnum. The Art of Money Getting (1880).

If you search the 'entrepreneurship' section on Amazon.co.uk you will find 24,736 publications. Rather than ploughing through that lot on a never-ending search for some business elixir, consider the three sentences my father, James Forte, a self-made entrepreneur, sent me the day I started my first business (see Appendix A for full transcript of this email).

- If you give someone a pound and they give you a pound and one penny, then you are in front.
- Know when you are losing money.
- Don't repeat the same mistake that caused the loss.

That's all you need to know (only kidding - a bit). The act of doing business has not changed in thousands of years and will never change. It is encapsulated in those three sentences. Only the tools that are available to facilitate those actions shift and develop with the advent of new technologies.

Rather than fuelling enterprise, the overload of noise created by the sea of business authors is strangling it. At best, it makes it confusing to know which way is right for you. At worst it's debilitating and demoralising to you as an entrepreneur as it fosters a cult of 'super entrepreneurs'. The media feed us a constant stream of business 'heroes' who willingly buy into the idea that they are better than us and must lead by example.

But what an example, where our young people are growing up with role models that appear to believe being a ruthless bastard is how to get on in business, with a media that fuels that myth in the name of entertainment! Anyone who runs a business knows that being rude to an employee or customer is a fast track to failure. We know a number of entrepreneurs who successfully won funding on Dragon's Den, and before they go on, the producers say 'have fun, it's only a television show'. It's not though. It's much more than that, as these shows are the often the first glimpse of business that young people get.

Information overload creates fog, not focus, for an entrepreneur. The peddling of a 'one best way' culture leads to linear thinking, not creativity. Believing people are better than you leads to doubt not inspiration. We reject all of the above. Buying into these ideas will turn you into a robot, following business by numbers, destined to be average not great. What gives us the right to question the merit of the current business book and media approach? We have history on our side.

P.T. Barnum – A Blast from the Past

In the 19th century, the author P.T. Barnum was the most successful entrepreneur of his generation, a legendary showman who became one of the wealthiest men in the world. Like Sugar he, too, started out with virtually nothing as a teenager. Ultimately his business toured the world and made his fortune.

Barnum was a pioneer in business and his claims to fame are many, including inventing outdoor advertising (maybe we shouldn't thank him for that). But as entrepreneurs, we should thank him for his *failure*.

Despite being one of the richest people in the World, Barnum, like the rest of us, was not immune to making a bad decision. In the early 1850s, he agreed to a venture with two unscrupulous business people who left Barnum owing a fortune. Despite facing bankruptcy, Barnum refused to default on his creditors, believing this act would ruin him in business for the rest of his life. His reputation depended on clearing his debts and he needed to create a new way to raise funds and repay his creditors, one that required minimal capital outlay, as his cash situation was dire.

From this dilemma, and out of desperate necessity, Barnum invented a completely new kind of business - the business seminar and workshop. Shorn of capital, Barnum penned a book entitled *The Art of Money Getting* and started touring the world, being paid to deliver the material in person to large groups of aspiring entrepreneurs. His popularity remained undiminished and he spent a decade raising funds through his appearances until finally clearing his former partners' debts.

In his autobiography, Barnum states that his family lived on beans and bread for many years throughout this period. Once free of the chains of debt, he immediately returned to showmanship and made a new fortune, becoming one of the wealthiest people in the world for a second time.

We don't tell you this story because we respect Barnum's integrity, his innovation or his tenaciousness (although we do). We share with you his story because, contrary to popular belief, nothing has changed. The mind set and disciplines needed to be a great entrepreneur 150 years ago are exactly the same today. Why would it be different? Human beings are still human beings.

The only difference is that rather than having to absorb the 36 pages in Barnum's book, we now have 2 billion. That's not progress.

We challenge you to read any book written on enterprise in the last 50 years that doesn't resemble his material and the learning in *The Art of Money Getting*. It's not intentional, malicious or anyone's fault, per se. It is just inevitable because the act of enterprise is simple and unchanged. People complicate.

Golden Rules for Money Making

P.T. Barnum told it like it is, explaining in simple terms the thinking and way of living that turned him into the Bill Gates of his time. He did this in as few as words as possible and didn't pad it out for self-serving reasons. He couldn't, because he was paid to stand up and deliver the material in person.

Thankfully, some things have changed since the 19th century and if you do read Barnum's book you will need to excuse the language of the day, particularly his views on women. However, the lessons in business remain invaluable and those are the words we embrace, while understanding that his values are those of his day which are not appropriate to today's world

Like Barnum, this book is the codification of a workshop, a seminar delivered to real businesses. What follows are snippets from *The Art of Money Getting*, written over one hundred years ago and proving that the art of enterprise is unchanged.

If you are going to read one book on business, *The Art of Money Getting* is it:

    1. Don't Mistake Your Vocation
"Unless you enter upon a vocation intended for you by nature, and best suited to your particular genius, you cannot succeed."

Message: It doesn't matter how good an entrepreneur you are, if you don't love your business and have an aptitude for it, you won't succeed.

2. Persevere

"It is this go-aheaditiveness, a determination not to let the horrors or the blues take possession of you, so as to make you relax your energies, which you must cultivate."

Message: Business is hard. You'll experience a new level of emotional pressure, one with deep peaks and troughs. Be relentless. Work on being positive.

3. Avoid Debt

"When interest is constantly piling up against you, it will keep you down in the worst kind of slavery."

Message: Don't borrow money if you don't have to. Debt attacks your mind, your enterprise and bank account – while you sleep.

4. Whatever You Do, Do It With All Your Might

"Do all you can for yourselves, and then trust to Providence or luck, or whatever you please to call it, for the rest."

Message: Only you can make it happen. No one is going to do it for you. That's reality. Relying on good fortune is not a plan. Execute violently.

5. Do Not Scatter Your Powers

"Engage in one kind of business only, stick to it faithfully until you succeed, or until your experience shows you should abandon it."

Message: Choosing what NOT to do is as important as deciding what to do in business. Be focused and single-minded in your goal.

6. Let Hope Predominate, But Be Not Too Visionary

"Many persons are kept poor because they are too visionary. Every project looks to them like a certain success, and therefore they keep changing, always in hot water, always under the harrow."

Message: If it isn't broken, don't fix it. You can have too many ideas. Once you have a clear vision, work on getting there, not creating a new one.

7. Be Charitable

"The liberal man will command patronage. The uncharitable miser will be avoided."

Message: It's not all about profit. Being helpful and kind in business is not just a selfless act, it is a powerful sales and marketing strategy.

8. Preserve Your Integrity

"It is more precious than diamonds."

Message: When you draw your last breath, integrity is all you will have left. Positivity and happiness boost your ability to be enterprising.

Why are we even telling you this?

When it comes to the act of business, nothing has changed since 1880.

The challenges that Barnum faced are the same as the ones we face. Don't complicate, be focused, execute violently and persevere. The only difference is that the world is faster and the resulting intensity of life, not business, is now the main barrier to success. As a result, *keep it simple to succeed* is even more relevant today than in Barnum's time, not less so.

Business is the easy part. Life is hard. As a business leader, a human being, the two are not separate. It is only by recognising and accepting this as fact, that work impacts on your life and vice versa, it is only then that you can become everything you want to be.

It is only then that you can Game Change your life in business.

ACT 1: KNOW YOURSELF

Chapter 1
What is a Future State?

Do you have one? An inherent sense of where you are going in business and why? The underlying and compelling reason why you get up in the morning and put yourself through all the trials and tribulations to grow a business? That sense of purpose that gets you through the tough times and lets you celebrate the good times, because you know everything is moving you closer to what you want to achieve in life (through business)?

We suspect you have never written that down. We never meet anyone who has written it down. Not in a concise way. Not it a way that makes it meaningful - a personal statement of intent and direction.

Yes, we see lots of written vision statements, mission statements and business plans. But if we were all being honest with ourselves, they're normally lengthy documents (more than a page!) that have been written with some investment of time and energy for someone else's purpose. That reason might be applying for funding, or 'my adviser told me I needed one', or 'everyone else seems to have one, so I must, too'. Don't misunderstand us, these documents have value in that they achieve an end and bring some semblance of process for people to follow. However, what do these documents really do for you - the leader of the business, the person who has to constantly create, innovate and energise everyone else? When did you last look at yours?

The business plan itself is an interesting construct, that business can be mechanical and measured and that everything must have a place. In our experience in business support, and we are sure yours as a business person, we know too well that any plan is out of date one hour after we write the full stop. The ink isn't even dry when something will come out of left field and change the challenges we face. That might be a new competitor, or it may be something more personal. That is the reason business plans and process driven thinking have such low credibility in the business community. They build in inflexibility and do not reflect the reality which we all face every day. As a result, the uncomfortable truth is the majority of these documents live in dark drawers or on dusty shelves, rather than at the heart of a business.

Your business journey doesn't conveniently follow a straight line. In reality it's a series of events, which cause peaks and troughs. Your success depends on how fast you recognise when you are pulled off the path, having the capability (and creativity) to do something to make an adjustment and return. In text books they call this *strategic drift*. In the real world we call it reacting, not leading.

When we meet an entrepreneur who has taken on a new contract because of profit, we always challenge them how this contributes to reaching their Future State in life, as quickly and economically as possible. You might be pleased to be making some short term profits but at what cost? Potentially, the bigger picture, your purpose and your life.

Put simply, the most common reason for strategic drift is deciding not to turn work away. That may sound crazy, but your most precious commodity as a leader is time. If you don't spend every single working second of your business day contributing to reaching your future state, you are behind. We don't care how much money you have made. We care about you achieving happiness in business and life. If any proof is needed, the majority of the wealthiest people we meet in business are miserable and unhappy. Yes, they have money but so what, because anyone who measures achievement in life in terms of money is a fool. No one has ever lain on their death bed and uttered with their final breath the words "I wish I'd worked more hours and made more money". That will never happen.

Therefore, every day lost to activities which do not contribute to your future state is a day lost to your life.

You must create your own measures of success, one's personal to you, your family and business. That's what we mean when we talk of your Future State. It must include life goals because that is why we put ourselves through the act of business in the first place; money in itself is just the bi-product.

Let's be clear on the meaning of enterprise. It's the act of creating something from nothing. You can complicate it if you want (and many do), but fundamentally when you strip it down and cut out all the hyperbole, that's your job as the leader of the business – to create opportunity. All the pressures of life and business will try and stop you doing this every day, and a life-long study of nuts and bolts business knowledge won't help you in that situation.

What you need is a simple framework and set of tools to keep you honest, to keep you believing and to keep you happy. Because if you can remain consistently driven and focused, success always follows.

You must decide your own future state, then do everything in your power to reach it, creating new strategies and opportunities, creating solutions to challenges and threats, and constantly driving forwards.

If you have that unwavering sense of purpose and the time to create, you will achieve your future state.

There is no text book 'one best way' to do this. You're a human being and that makes you unique. One size does not fit all, however much people want you to believe it. In this book we share with you the way we have witnessed to be most effective.

Your Future Statement

At the heart of your business must be your life. That means every time you aspire to a sales target, or new project, you're doing so to reach an end game, a future state. This statement of your future must have three vital components to be effective. It has to be:

Qualitative – life drives business not the other way round, even though you can't measure happiness

You need to describe what your perfect existence is. That may be spending more time with your children, or grandchildren. It could be travelling. It might be starting a new business. Whatever it is, it's something you can't do yet for many reasons, often financial, sometimes emotional (fulfilment). If you are already in that place, congratulations. We know you're not though, otherwise you wouldn't be reading this book.

When we speak to the leaders of businesses they all start describing how they wish they could spend more time living and less time working. They wish their lives weren't so filled with stress and pressure. They want to be happier. We think that's a pretty reasonable set of demands!

Process and business by numbers will not get you to this place because life is not mathematics.

Instead the solution lies in how you think, how you feel and how you live your values. These are soft measures, not hard measures, but we live in a business culture that says if you can't measure it, you can't manage it, so don't do it. We don't agree with that philosophy.

Those 25,000 books on enterprise; in a generation they haven't made a single dent in the most depressing statistic in business. On average, more than half of start-up businesses fail within five years in the United Kingdom. Fewer than two-thirds survive their first three years.

These figures are not an anomaly. The Government's own statistics evidence that, over the past twenty years, the failure rate has rarely shifted more than a couple of per cent. Worse still, business survival is on the decline (see Appendix B).

It's not for lack of effort. Successive Governments have tried in vain to shift this figure by investing in business support. More than most, we know first-hand that all entrepreneurs try their utmost to succeed. And it's not for lack of training, as billions have been invested by both Government and private sector.

Therefore, simple logic says that it must be the wrong kind of training. Look at the statistics; the survival rate of businesses doesn't lie. That level of performance is the output of all that investment. If you want to continue to follow the 'business by numbers' path, then accept that your chances of success are less than half.

We don't like those odds.

If you want to improve your chances then you are going to have to do something different, do something Game Changing.

The truth is that when you remove life from the business equation, when cataclysmic events occur and the proverbial hits the fan (and it will), in our experience the majority of business leaders are unprepared to deal with these situations. They may well know how to read a set of accounts, to improve systems and recruit people, but that won't save your business in these stretch moments. In those situations, *you* are the only person that can do that.

To achieve long-term success, you must go above and beyond in terms of your commitment and creativity, not just in the good times, but also in the worst of times. You will only do that if you can see a light at the end of the tunnel, a better life for your family, for your friends, for happiness. Not just for money.

That is why your future state must describe what your perfect life in business looks like, what you want to be doing in your ideal world – in and out of work. There are no rules on this; no consultant or anyone else can tell you the answers, as it's your life.

It's a blank sheet of paper. You decide.

<u>Quantitative</u>

Your future state is just wishful thinking without financial foundations.

You've taken the first step; you've written down a destination, but that's not enough. After aspiration comes perspiration, and if you are going to exert effort in the right places on your journey, you need to know you are on track. That means milestones and markers. Your task is to create, not wildly and without direction, but with focus and application.

That means you now need to translate those life goals into business goals. How much money does your business need to support that ideal life? How much time do you need away from day-to-day business to spend with the kids? These are quantitative financial measures. Profit. Time. Asset value.

By quantifying your life challenge in business terms, you then create a framework that everyone can understand and contribute to. Of course not everyone wants to know you plan to sell the business, but you want the people around you to contribute to that goal. They only need to know the target.

Business growth for business sake is a far less powerful driver than goals linked to a happy ending.

For all intents and purposes they are the same financial and quantitative targets you may see in any other business. However, in reality they are entirely different, as these measures are derived from your aspiration, not a 'must grow for growth's sake' mentality. They mean more and you take them more seriously. If your life plan required you to make 25% net profit and you make 20%, your accountant may be delighted, but you shouldn't be. Because you know you're behind the pace of the plan. That means arriving later, costing you that time with the family. You shouldn't be satisfied and must double your efforts.

When you use a Future Statement you know that achieving quantitative milestones in themselves means something much more than financial gain. It's a reality check, a benchmark against which you can test your decisions. If it doesn't contribute to the bigger picture, why do it? The answer is you shouldn't.

Don't misunderstand us; without a Future Statement you may still arrive in a happy place years down the road (half don't; sorry, it's a fact). However, you don't know what it will be so you can't influence your ideal existence. You have far more chance of creating your desired future state if you write down what the business must be doing financially to support your life. That means you own it.

Your future statement must include a financial measure of performance, what the business looks like at the end game. If not, your future state is just built on wishful thinking, not financial foundations. As an entrepreneur your challenge is to create the exact set of accounts you need.

Time-based

A target without a deadline is just a dream.

Tell us the month and year you want to reach this position in your life and business. It may be ten years down the line, but we want to know. *You* need to know every single day. That's what focus is.

If you don't put a deadline in it, you're not under pressure, you have less purpose, less drive, less focus. Your decisions are unchallenged as there is less urgency. Time makes you and your business, everyone in your business, accountable to each other. You know if you arrived when you said you would.

If your plan is to retire in five years' time and it takes eight, that's three years of your life you'll never get back, be it with your family or doing whatever you love. That's the cost of strategic drift: life. The average life expectancy is 80. Failure to arrive on time, in this scenario, costs you 5 percent of your life (3 years), the quality bit too. That really focuses the mind, every day.

KEEP IT SIMPLE TO SUCCEED

When writing your Future Statement, you need to be brief and succinct. Avoid being generic, be specific and not limiting but above all, it needs to be personal to you.

Three sentences – what is your ideal life, what does that equate to financially, and when do you want to be there (not how)?

Your Future Statement = Qualitative + Quantitative + Time-Based

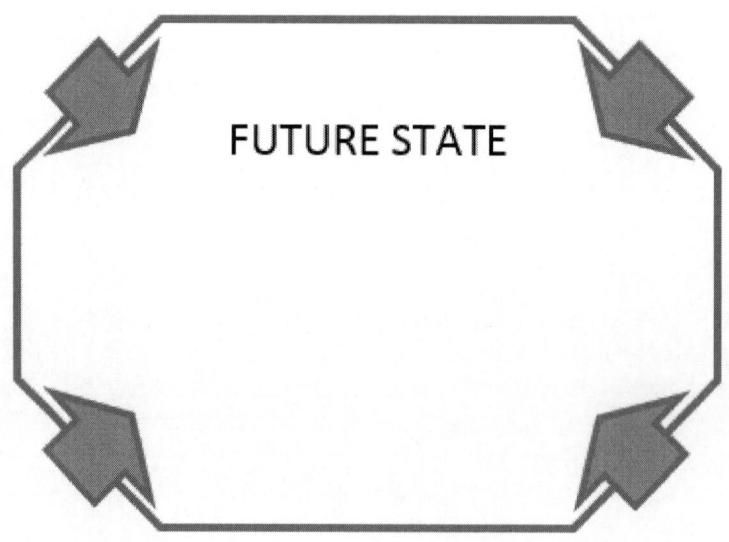

If you can't make your future state fit in this box, it's still too complicated.

Need some help? See 'Appendix C' for real business examples.

Don't need to write it down? You already know where you're going?

"Writing things down has four major advantages.

First, it takes all those fleeting worries and makes them concrete so you can see them and deal with them.

Second, it makes it possible to see connections and consolidate tasks.

Third, it lets you look at some of those things and let them go. Yes, I need to plan my sabbatical. But not today. I can put that off for a month or two and it will still be ok.

Most importantly, if everything is written down you don't have to keep thinking about it. Rehearsal is the process of saying something over and over so you don't forget it. One of the reasons we keep returning to things and worrying about them is that we're rehearsing: we are returning to the same idea over and over so we don't forget it. If we write it down and trust that we won't forget it, we can stop rehearsing it.

No open loop. No recurring thought. *Lower anxiety*."

Psychology Today, 2015

You're also going to have to bring a lot of people with you on the journey to make your Future Statement a reality, because you can't do it all by yourself. These people need to understand how they contribute to the business journey and success. They need to be singing from the same hymn sheet, not buying into a Chinese whisper.

If that's not enough to persuade you, personally we always choose to avoid a dose of avoidable anxiety. Business and life are stressful enough!

It's your life, you decide.

Chapter 2
Constructing Your Future State Template

Let's revisit the purpose of this entire exercise. To be the best entrepreneur you can be, you must have an inherent and instinctive understanding of:

- WHY you put yourself through the act of business in the first place (life aspiration)

- WHAT you are trying to create – what the business will look and feel like to work in once your journey is complete

- WHEN you must get to this destination

Those three sentences create a potent force to be drive you on because they fuel ABOVE and BEYOND purpose.

You see more opportunity as you constantly live in the bigger picture. It means you push yourself harder than you realised was possible, as everything you do is not just for yourself, it's for the people you love. It compels you to create more opportunities and counter threats, because you know the clock is constantly ticking and a day lost to the business journey is a day lost to your life.

In the previous chapter, you were asked to fill in the middle of the Future State Template – the Future Statement. However, that is not enough to make your hopes and dreams a reality. We now need to define and articulate the strategically important actions that ensure you arrive at the right place at the right time.

Once you have defined what is critically important, you must then make sure this information never leaves your sight, because that is how a plan becomes instinctive, by rehearsal. Display the document on the wall of your offices so it is constantly in sight, absorbed every time you walk past. Carry it in your case, so that you see it every time you open a folder to do day-to-day actions. Make sure the Future State is the first thing you look at before starting any discussions on strategy, for example a Board meeting or a session with partners or your family.

It is only by performing this 'eyes on' repetition that your business and life goals become embedded in your psyche and become second nature to you. Once that has happened your capability to be a successful entrepreneur will soar because all your decision making becomes more focused and targeted.

For practical reasons the Future State Template must be no more than one page of A4 in length. Any longer and you need to stop and turn the page. That requires effort. It increases the time to consume the information and it complicates understanding. As a result, you become far less likely to perform the act of rehearsal.

Even in the most complicated businesses we have worked with, regardless of turnover, the leaders have always managed to encapsulate their strategy in this concise focused way.

That means you can do it, too.

Introducing Strategically Important Action (SIA)

Your mind has to process tens of thousands of decisions every day.

Business is an incredibly complex web of relationships linking people, materials, behaviour and money. Your role as a business leader is to be mindful of these relationships and create plans to improve their output. If we visit Amazon.co.uk today, there are 2 million business books on the shelf trying to unravel and demystify the nuts and bolts of creating, selling, delivering and financing customer demand. However, even though there are thousands of decisions to consider in your daily business life, there will be only a handful that truly have strategic impact (critical to the future of the business), the remainder are tactically important (important, but not critical).

In reality the majority of your decisions will be tactical, low impact, meaning they don't really matter. If you focus the majority of your energy and time on improving these tactical actions it will be virtually impossible to arrive at your Future State, certainly not in the time intended.

Therefore, the biggest threat to realising your Future State is always you.

Strategically Important Action (SIA) differs fundamentally from tactical because these areas of the business are absolutely critical to realising your future state.

You must invest time, energy and money into these bigger picture actions, not just in brief bursts but constantly, or the future state will fail.

We call these elements of your business the CORE CONTRIBUTORS and there are four that can generate strategically important impact.

BRAND / SALES   PROCESS   PEOPLE   MONEY

When you invest in strategically important actions within these pressure points the results are exponential, powering up performance and accelerating the journey towards your Future State.

Feel Good Failure

Roughly 80% of the effects come from 20% of the causes.

Complicate it as much as you want, but the Pareto Principle is the difference between successful entrepreneurs and those who fail to realise their goals.

You only have a finite amount of time you can invest as a business leader. Time is the only asset in business that you can't grow with the investment of money. You can buy in other people's time, improve capability with training, but it will always be impossible to create more than 24 hours of time in your *own* day. If you focus on elements of the business that have a low impact, consciously or subconsciously, you generate a low impact gain. In business, you cannot afford to make a mistake when deciding where to focus your energy.

If you are right more times than wrong, then the business is a success and you realise your Future Statement.

Therefore, knowing the Core Contributors in your business is not a 'nice to have' piece of information. That knowledge is absolutely critical to your life and future. You must have absolute certainty where the positive pressure points are in your business i.e., those actions that produce exponential gain. It's the only way to know if you are working hard but bleeding opportunity.

This challenge is further exacerbated by the daily pressures of business that you are certain to face. During the working day, every bone in your body will be yearning to pull you into a tactical firefight, rather than to think strategically. Tactical issues manifest themselves to us obviously and immediately. It is not difficult to recognise when there's a dissatisfied customer or when a supplier is failing to deliver. The tangible short-term gain or loss is presented clearly to us. You can see the immediate benefit and react accordingly. However, when you consider you are the only person who can make the Future State a reality, this is a false economy; better to delegate and trust others to resolve the situation. Or if you are a sole trader, better to deal with this one time and make changes in the business to ensure it never happens again. That is the dilemma you will face every day. We agree that every decision in business is important. However, we don't accept the idea that all of them are strategically important. You must protect your time.

This is the primary reason that entrepreneurs reach a plateau in performance and struggle to break through turnover ceilings. Whilst the business leader may be an excellent manager, that focus can only take you so far. To achieve your Future State someone must always be looking ahead to steer the business. If that's not you, who is it?

The answer is no one. That means the business is drifting (forwards hopefully) and has no clear direction.

Do not misunderstand us; we know too well the day-to-day pressures that running a business can put upon you and there will always be a tactical issue where you must get involved. However, that should be the exception not the rule.

The Future State Template acts as your compass and a reality-check to return to each day, keeping you honest in both your actions and thinking.

In this way, by being constantly and acutely aware of the bigger picture, that means that you know that a successful day in the office can actually be an unsuccessful day in business i.e., if your actions didn't contribute to realising the Future State, you made money not progress.

In that context your actions are in reality a *feel good failure*.

You'll need to get back on track.

Why Pick Just Four?

We advocate isolating just four strategically important actions because that is the number that it is feasible to power up - economically and mentally. Any more and you will be stretching yourself thinner and focus will dilute.

We are acutely aware that this approach is contrary to the current thinking on how to improve business. The plethora of books and business support initiatives are still entrenched in the ideals of performance management - act, measure, review and revise. To demonstrate how ineffective this approach can be when it comes to enterprise, let us revisit two recent Government flagship initiatives which attempted to productise leading and directing a business.

SIBBP – death by measurement

In 2004 the Government launched Support to Implement Business Best Practice, a benchmarking tool intended to help leaders focus on what really matters in their organisation. This scheme challenged the leaders of businesses to accurately measure a total of 75 factors across the business.

The number of organisations that actually had capability to access that level of management information was minimal and while, theoretically, this should support excellent decision-making, in reality it failed to achieve the desired impact because of incomplete data and the sheer scale of information to process.

It is a business by numbers approach that believes process, not enterprise, is the route to success. It makes no attempt to improve your business acumen.

Incidentally, this project cost the Government £44 million to roll out and we refer you to the earlier statistic - 55% of businesses still fail within 5 years. Not even a dent.

Accelerator

At the time of writing, the most recent Government funded scheme to transform business performance was called Growth Accelerator, part of the Business Growth Service. This initiative was shut down in November 2015.

It had at its heart the Vision Orbit model, a solid performance management methodology that has merit when you need to bring structure out of chaos. However, once again there was minimal attempt to address the enterprise deficit. The scheme still held onto the principles of performance management but stripped down to a 'vital few' measures.

Vision Orbit is an excellent strategy mapping tool, but we would argue that it chokes your ability to be flexible and creative – and that is what you need to be competitive in a rapidly changing business environment.

While an improvement on SIBBP, the methodology was still too complex and detailed to create any enterprise capital. Vision Orbit is an effective management tool, but it is still too process-driven to stimulate enterprise.

As we have stated previously, *you* are the most precious asset in your business and all the process in the world will not save you from the 55% failure rate, unless you can be the best entrepreneur you can be.

Furthermore, over a 5-year-period, these initiatives were targeted to engage 46,000 businesses out of five million, just 1% of the business population.

Source:

Growth Accelerator Annual Report for 2012 – 2014
http://www.ga.businessgrowthservice.greatbusiness.gov.uk

Interim Evaluation of Growth Accelerator, BIS Research Paper No. 187, page 10, November 2014

That level of intervention will help a lucky few but will make no significant impact on the survival rate of entrepreneurs.

If you want to have a one in two chance of surviving five years in business, then buy into the same approach. If you want a better chance, you must do something that is *different*.

Introducing Core Contributors

The number of strategically important actions number only four because that's a lot more realistic for you to own and make sense of. Due to its brevity and focus, the Future State Template is a working tool that you can refer to every day, one that guides your decision-making every time and gives you the room to be entrepreneurial.

We don't think becoming a robot is a great business strategy. It may seem a safer option, but being yourself is the key to being an entrepreneur, not following a matrix of measures. That's what managers do.

Of course, if you are a sole trader you will have no managers. You will have to be both an entrepreneur and a manager.

Set aside specific time to manage – don't let it become your default state. It's more comfortable to be a manager than an entrepreneur.

The Core Contributors approach also has one other significant advantage over existing tools – you don't need a PhD to make it work! To Game Change your performance only demands you follow a simple sequence of four steps.

1. Check Future State
2. Did you invest energy in all the Core Contributors today?
3. If not, why not?
4. If no good reason (being busy or making profit are not good reasons), that's a fail - do something about it tomorrow.

That's the measurement over with. You stay on course and move forward.

If the Pareto Principle applies, and we all breathe the same air so it definitely does, reducing the business failure rate won't be achieved by improving the nuts and bolts processes that make up the act of business. Instead it will come from inspiring and improving the focus and enterprise capability of people like you, the leaders directing businesses.

With Directors, boardrooms and businesses, our approach is always the same; fix the top and the rest will follow. That's why you only have four Core Contributors to achieve your future state.

It just isn't more complicated than that. Feel free to create some more measures if you feel the need to. As always, you decide. They will certainly help you look back and see how you've done, but they won't help you look forward. Be conscious that every new challenge you add dilutes your focus and spreads your energy thinner.

That decision reduces your competitive advantage.

A Glimpse at the Future State Template

At the end of this book you will have constructed your own personal and unique Future State Template. However, before we move onto building the grid, it is vital that you know that you, the entrepreneur, are fit for purpose.

As the only person who can make your Future State a reality, you need to know you're ready to do it.

We need you to *know yourself* in business and your current enterprise capability (good and bad) or the Future State will fail.

Chapter 3
Business Life and Death

Before you can know yourself as an entrepreneur, it is vital you understand a fundamental law of business.

If you keep doing the same thing, everything fails in the end.

It is inevitable and that is why we need you to be enterprising every single day.

The Most Important Curve in Business

The business life cycle is the same for every organisation on the planet, bar none.

PHASE 1: CREATE LIFE

Strategy: <u>Sales and marketing</u> to create demand.

On one hand, this is the most exciting time for any entrepreneur.

On the other, it is the most stressful as the business is inherently fragile at the outset, success is uncertain and relies heavily on your ability to create life through enterprise.

Every entrepreneur should treasure and remember this time, as it is when you are most powerful as an entrepreneur because you risk only your launch money and personal pride.

That should empower you, not inhibit you.

When a business starts up, the overriding strategy must be to secure customers, to generate sales and revenue.

Without money, the life blood of every company, it doesn't matter how brilliant your product or service may be or how good your people are. It is imperative that customers are persuaded to pay you - fast.

Products never sell themselves.

Any other focus at this stage in the business life cycle will lead to failure. Marketing and sales strategies must dominate.

If you don't have the capability to create a winning sales strategy, it is critical you find someone who can.

PHASE 2: SUSTAIN LIFE

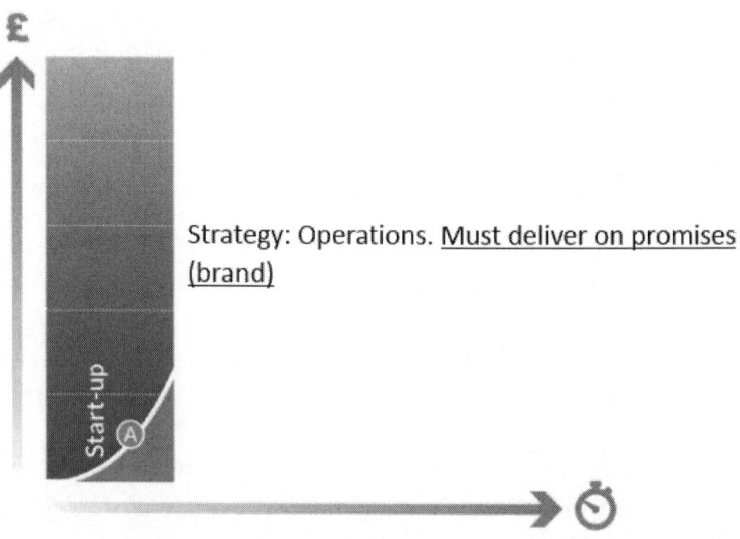

Strategy: Operations. Must deliver on promises (brand)

Sales breed more sales. Customers tell their friends, word of mouth builds and your reputation grows.

Once you have lit the touch paper then there is a different challenge to overcome in business; keeping customers delighted, and we mean *delighted*, not just happy.

Delighting customers is not complicated. You keep them informed, you deliver what you promise, at a time of their choosing, and you check they're smiling at the end.

Once again, complicate it more if you wish but that is fundamentally the process of customer fulfilment.

This means it's time for an operational strategy, one that improves systems and processes, incorporates controls and checks and ensures you invest the resources needed to make good on the ever-increasing demands on your business.

The business must keep delivering all the things you would expect if you were a customer. If you don't get this right first time, you could kill your business before it even gets going.

Businesses die if they break their brand promise. People talk, especially in the age of social media.

Make sure they say nice things.

PHASE 3: PAYBACK

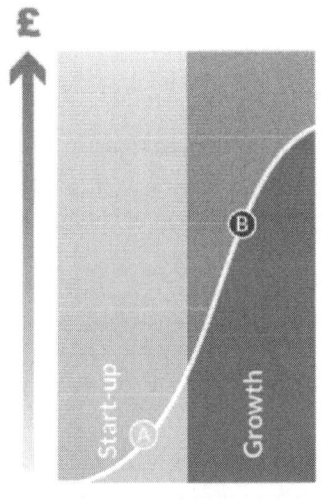

Strategy: Finance pace of growth (don't run out of cash) and investment in infrastructure and people i.e., capability to service rapidly growing demand.

At this stage, your hard work is paying off big time. Customers are happy and the business has momentum.

In fact, success is turning out to be the biggest headache you've encountered in business so far. You are having to invest in ever-increasing resources in terms of people and infrastructure to service your order book and keep the brand promise intact.

Demand is increasing exponentially and that means you are having to hold more stock and are starting to incur more labour costs as you need more people to deliver the service levels that customers expect.

This payback period looks fantastic on paper in money terms, but the reality is that this is when most entrepreneurs fail, as they have not implemented timely financial strategies.

Rapid growth is a serious threat to your Future State.

Everything listed above costs money.

If you are fortunate enough to be paid by customers at the point of sale, then the impact is less as your business is effectively self-financing (or should be). However, the majority of entrepreneurs now face a cash squeeze on their business as they are forced to finance an ever increasing number of transactions, before delivery and payment.

History is littered with entrepreneurs who had profitable products and business models, but their organisations fell over because there was insufficient cash available to maintain supply.

In a bid to survive this shortfall, businesses are often forced into delaying delivery, laying off staff, reducing spending on marketing, effectively committing commercial suicide.

Timely financial strategies are critical to ensure you aren't a victim of your own hard earned success.

PHASE 4: PEAKING

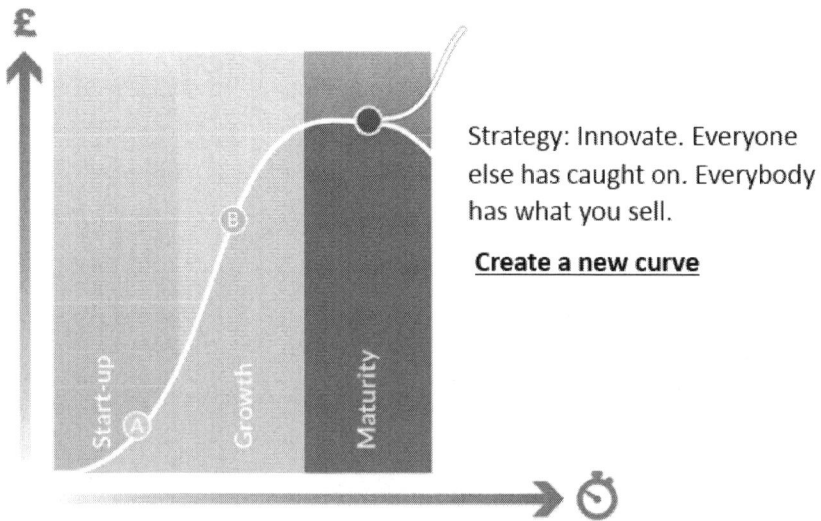

Strategy: Innovate. Everyone else has caught on. Everybody has what you sell.

Create a new curve

Now you really have to earn your money because your venture is about to die.

When you first launched your offering, there was a gap in the market and latent demand. You enjoyed the spoils of your enterprise as customers swarmed to your business. However, the market has become more competitive over time as other entrepreneurs have seen the opportunity and entered the market.

Competitors have introduced substitutes for customers to pick from. In tandem, the potential market itself is likely to be shrinking (unless your product is a necessity that fosters repeat purchase). The number of people who need your product or service is falling as more and more customers already own it.

Every market becomes saturated in time.

It is during this period (earlier ideally) that you must *create a new curve*, an innovation that changes the business direction and generates new opportunities, for example, new products or adaptations to the existing offer or entering new markets. Or, in other words, a whole new enterprise. You're back in phase one – create life and start selling again.

PHASE 5: DECLINE TO DEATH

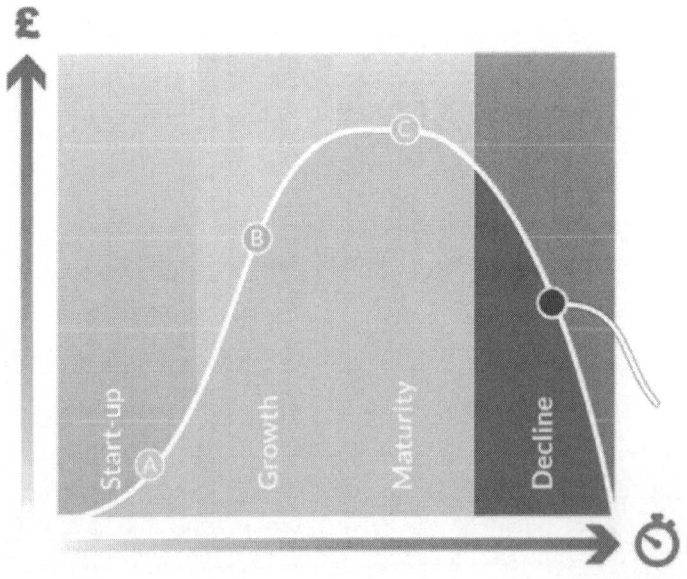

If you find yourself in this position, your back is against the wall. You have failed to create a 'new curve' in time and the revenue in your business is falling rapidly. There is now a cash shortfall available for investment in innovation. Everyone knows it – the bank, your customers, your suppliers, competitors and staff - especially your staff.

You now run the risk that you may lose your best people.

A chain of events is underway that is extremely difficult to alter because your choices are now limited. In many cases the only option is to achieve a soft landing.

You can diversify and open up a completely new kind of business, abandoning the current course completely. Alternatively, you can exit through business sale or voluntary closure (evacuation).

Whichever strategy you employ, the return on your investment (usually many years) is not what it should have been. The sale price of your business is lower because the profits are reduced and the market is saturated. The best scenario in closure is to emerge debt-free, if you can find a buyer at all at this stage - most don't. Even diversification is effectively a re-start, sacrificing your past efforts.

You do not want to find yourself in the 'Decline to Death' scenario, at the end of the business life cycle with your Future State in tatters.

To this end, it is a critical part of your role as an entrepreneur to ensure you implement the right strategies at the right time.

KEEP IT SIMPLE TO SUCCEED

Plot your monthly net profit from start up to current day. Is the trend upwards or downwards? Where do you think your organisation is on the Business Life Cycle curve? Are you employing the right strategies?

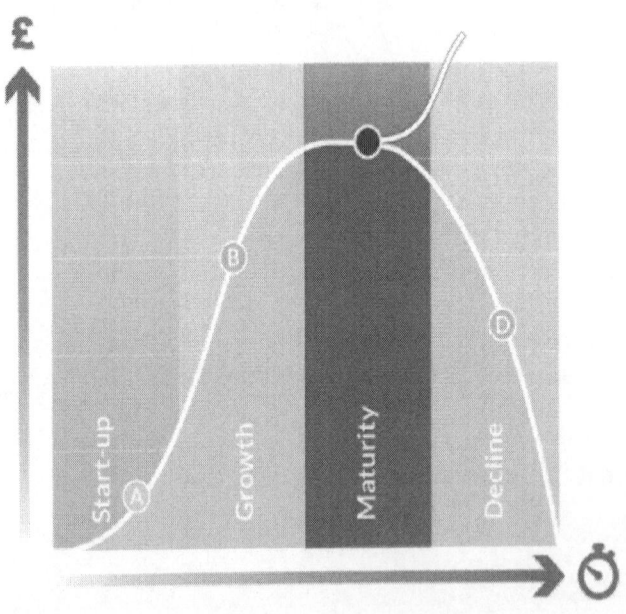

Start: Create Life	**Sales and marketing** to create demand.
A: Sustain Life	Must **deliver on promises** (brand) – **operations**.
B: Payback	**Finance** pace of growth (don't run out of cash).
C: Peaking	Competitors caught up. Innovate: **Create a new curve** (rebirth).
D: Decline to Death	No time to innovate. Must rapidly **diversify** or plan for **exit**.

If it hasn't already, when do you think your business will reach the *Peaking* phase? Why? What can you do about it?

The Coca Cola Challenge

In a recent Game Change workshop one of the participants challenged the inevitability of the decline to death principle, citing the example of Coca Cola as a business that has lasted in excess of 100 years and shows no signs of decline.

Our answer to this is simple and short.

Coca Cola is an innovative company that constantly creates new curves in terms of markets and brands, rather than the product itself. However, even with their huge resources they will ultimately fail and succumb to competition.

When it comes to the business life cycle, the only difference between us and an organisation such as Coca Cola is the length of the curve.

Typically, when entrepreneurs decide to continue doing the same thing and fail to innovate, the decline to death period is 3 to 5 years. The business life cycle curve at Coca Cola could be 500 years!

Ultimately, they will decline to death. No business is immortal.

To reach your future state, it's imperative you have the focus and time needed to create the *right* strategy at the *right* time.

Chapter 4
Prime Driver

Just in case you're in any doubt, when it comes to who is the prime driver in your business, we can confirm unequivocally that it is always you.

You are the only person who can make your Future State a reality and that means you need to be at the top of your game, not in short bursts, but every single second of every single day.

Unfortunately, you're not a robot; hence, the challenge. That means you're going to have to self-regulate as an entrepreneur. That's far from a painless experience.

Know Yourself

You don't. We don't. It's impossible. Can we be any clearer than that?

However, if you fail to know yourself in terms of your capability to be enterprising, then two massive threats to your Future State come into play. These states of mind are the catalyst for poor business decisions, unnecessary risk taking and ultimately underachievement (or even failure).

Unconscious Overconfidence

Your decisions in business must be entrepreneurial at all times, but they must also be astute. That means that you must be acutely aware of your environment (including life) and the emotions that give you too much belief, that take you from the mind set of calculated risk to blind faith. If we rely too much on chance, eventually we will fail as entrepreneurs. In Casinos, the House always beats the gambler. You can only win in the long-term if you know your limitations and count the cards, making decisions based on probability of success, not hope.

Unconscious Doubt

This state of mind is actually even more damaging because at least blind faith can sometimes work, if only more by luck than judgement. When it comes to unconscious doubt it never works. It causes a decision-making paralysis or over-cautiousness which restricts your ability to be enterprising. There's no 'might work' scenario in this state, as it is effectively built-in under-achievement. When you are in this place mentally, your decisions are low impact because you have become so risk averse. By being less entrepreneurial, your decisions fail to create enough value and, whilst safer, the impact is insufficient. That means your future state moves further away every day and actually becomes a road to nowhere, even though outwardly you appear to have momentum.

It is not a weakness to recognise that the act of business is as much dependent on your mental state as your physical actions. Once you accept this to be the case, then we all need help to understand (with any meaning) where we are mentally at any given time.

Alone, it is impossible to truly know yourself.

How will I know?

Not easily.

The first step is to understand how the business life cycle can force changes to your mentality. Your perception of risk and reward will come under new pressures as your business grows. Your belief in return on investment is the very principle that underpins entrepreneurial thinking and enterprise.

If you unconsciously become risk-averse, your decisions change. If you become bullish because everything seems to be working, your decisions change. That will only work for so long in business, if at all.

While we encourage every entrepreneur to be enthusiastic and happy, that should not be at the cost of reason. As business leaders we need to be unemotional when we test the merits of different scenarios and decisions.

That's the way we avoid making rash decisions.

There are two primary influencers on your entrepreneurial state. The first is emotions triggered by your experiences at work. The second is emotions triggered by events in your personal life. Regardless of where these events take place, the impact of these triggers is always personal.

The extent of your reaction is determined by your life position and how you feel about it. In poker terminology, these events effectively put you 'on tilt' as an entrepreneur.

'Tilt' is a poker term for a state of mental or emotional confusion or frustration in which a player adopts a less than optimal strategy, usually resulting in the player becoming erratic and making poor decisions. The player does not realise they are on tilt; it is an unconscious state of mind. The player on tilt always loses in the end because those around him are making calculated decisions, based on the cold reality of probability - risk and reward. They win more times than they lose.

Tilt is the perfect analogy for what you will face on a daily basis because it's your job to ensure you win more times than you lose.

The reality is all entrepreneurs experience tilt, many times every day. That's the nature of life, it's unpredictable and stressful. Our performance as entrepreneurs is as much linked to how fast we correct these emotional pulls, as it is to being creative.

Staying in the optimal enterprise zone is guaranteed to accelerate our journey to the Future State because we make better decisions and avoid deviation.

Maslow and its Impact on Enterprise

A key determinant of your ability to be entrepreneurial is the ability to think ahead and be visionary. You cannot be creative and enterprising if you are unable to do this effectively.

Maslow's well-trodden 'hierarchy of needs' was created to illustrate the motivational drivers for people, everyone, not just business leaders. However, if we flip the Maslow pyramid and substitute needs for attainment, then this is a far more effective illustration of the way thinking changes as entrepreneurs progress through their lives in business.

The diagrams that follow illustrate how your level of attainment is directly linked to your emotional capability to be enterprising (risk and reward).

Personal Drivers

Selflessness

Esteem

Reward

Security

Survival

Business Drivers

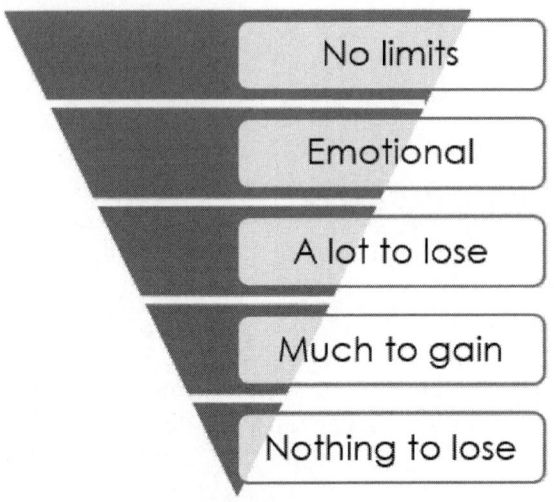

- No limits
- Emotional
- A lot to lose
- Much to gain
- Nothing to lose

Entrepreneurial Influence

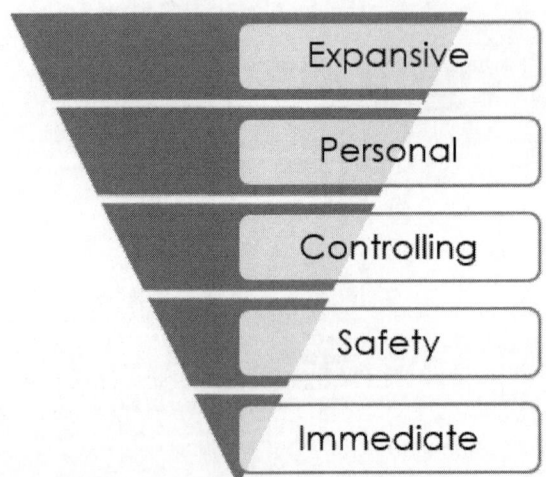

- Expansive
- Personal
- Controlling
- Safety
- Immediate

Level 1: SURVIVAL

+ Influence: Nothing to lose is a fearless mind-set and your focus on creation will never be higher.

- Influence: Short term objectives means sights are set low, stress levels are high and there is a tendency to get stuck in a perpetual firefight.

When you have very little attainment, your primary driver is survival.

In business terms, that means your mindset is by necessity tactical, your goal being to generate the minimum needed in the short-term to survive.

It is extremely difficult and challenging to look a year ahead when your income doesn't pay the bills. It's counter-intuitive to do so, but that is precisely what you must do to remain in an optimal enterprise state.

You self-regulate to discipline yourself to ignore this reality.

Level 2: SECURITY

+ Influence: Much to gain still, so highly motivated and still willing to speculate to accumulate.

- Influence: A growing 'safety first' mentality fostering a tendency towards consolidation and not creation.

Once you start to earn more, your primary driver becomes security.

You want to have the peace of mind that your income is sustainable and that your family is secure. Your ability to see into the future is increasing because you are less stressed and your mind is under less day-to-day assault. However, you are still thinking short-term, because your business is not yet generating consistent results. You have more to lose which breeds caution.

Level 3: REWARD

+ Influence: You have created both attainment and stability - stress levels should fall

- Influence: You now have a lot to lose and the tendency is to be controlling and risk averse – the business plateaus.

When you begin generating significant pay back, your natural instinct is to reward yourself and family for all your exertions.

You now have more freedom and time to think expansively, but much more to lose.

Your sense of achievement fosters an idea that your way is the right way and leads to a closed mind.

Level 4: ESTEEM

+ Influence: You are highly motivated as emotional drivers push you, not monetary ones.

- Influence: May take your eye off the bottom line. Risk-based decisions not being tested against return on investment.

It is only when you have all the money you need that you reach a pure entrepreneurial state.

At this stage in your life in business you are motivated by esteem. There is nothing more powerful than emotional drivers.

You are innovative as you are not driven by financial gain. Apathy may set in as business as usual has become boring.

Level 5: SELFLESSNESS

+ Influence: Everything you do is to progress the business and the people within it. Limitless ambition.

- Influence: Unfortunately, this state doesn't exist in the real World!

Entrepreneurial thinking unhindered by life influences.

A State of Denial

If striving for the optimal enterprise state, your most daunting challenge will be to train yourself to ignore personal profiteering as an entrepreneur, even though your life is screaming at you to do the opposite.

Only then are you able to see opportunities and threats most clearly, when you serve the business and not vice versa.

Doing this can be extremely difficult as you effectively force yourself to forgo a number of opportunities for short term gain, accepting short term pain to maintain an optimal entrepreneurial state. But that is how you *game change* business performance and realise your future state.

Note that this doesn't mean ignoring the finances, quite the reverse!

It is vital you hold a clear and up to date understanding of your financial position. After all, you must still be in the game to win it and there's little consolation in remaining strategic but going bust. If that means parking the plan for a moment, do it.

Beware the Wall

On your 'life in business' journey, you will inevitably reach a crossroads. During the reward phase, when you are generating payback for your early efforts and sacrifices, your level of attainment will start to influence your motivation. As stated previously, the tendency will be to reap the fruits of your endeavours.

You will then have to make a conscious choice - accept that this is as far as you want to go in business or press on towards your Future State. There's no wrong or right choice, it's your life - but be aware that for most people, realising their Future State means going beyond this emotional wall.

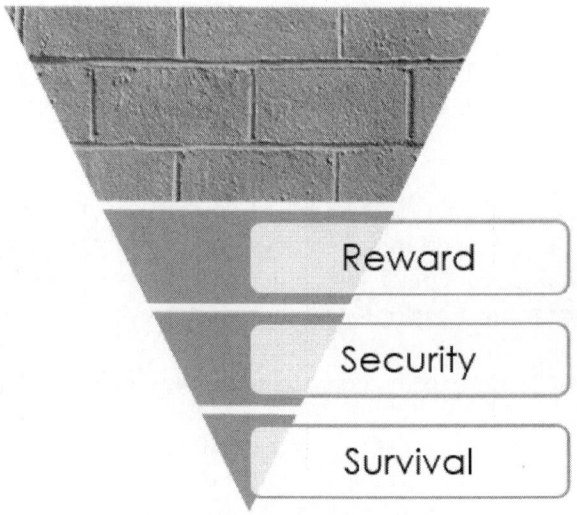

Future States created by entrepreneurs require a positive financial exit to fund their ideal life. That may be a business sale or it may be creating a standalone business that does not require your daily input, that runs itself and generates you income while you sleep.

In the first scenario, optimising the value of a business sale requires leaving the value in the company accounts, paying more tax than you would usually have to, so you can evidence profit potential and demonstrate you are not integral to maintaining levels of performance. Taking money out and exerting too much control are in direct conflict with asset-building, as this will keep the business dependent on you.

In the second scenario, you must generate a surplus of profit to fund the value you currently bring to the business. In our experience individual business owners and entrepreneurs typically do the workload equivalent of two employed personnel. That's not anything to be proud of. We are yet to witness a Future State that says I want to work 90 hour weeks and get paid half a salary.

Again, you have a choice. Accept that you will be involved with the business full time, working hard indefinitely but that you and your family can enjoy the rewards that brings. Or, reject that mentality and remain purely enterprising – a calculated risk-taker.

If you don't arrive at your Future State then at least you've done so by design and you won't be looking for excuses and others to blame. After all, ultimately the journey is all down to you. That's the greatest and worst part of being an entrepreneur. You decide your own destiny, no one else.

Either way, be in no doubt you had a choice and be happy with where you landed.

Chapter 5
Maintain an Enterprise State

Your life position is a powerful influence on your mind-set and behaviour in the long term. However, it is the catalogue of events and challenges you face every day that diminishes your capability to be enterprising in the short term.

We simply don't buy into the idea that entrepreneurs are born and that there is some genetic lottery that produces great business leaders.

In reality, you have to work hard to develop the skills and mindset needed to perform the role effectively.

If you do not have a deep understanding of the mindsets needed at the heart of enterprise, how can you maintain that state of mind?

Studying all the different theories for a lifetime is not the answer.

You will be in a permanent state of contradiction on what is and isn't the best approach.

In the ideal world, you would have time to work it out for yourself, working alongside good (and bad) entrepreneurs, observing how they think and act when it comes to improving business performance.

Unfortunately, unless you're a business consultant, you don't have that luxury.

We want to share with you our own beliefs, developed after observing and working first-hand with business leaders.

Enterprise is Elemental...

Let's revisit our definition of an entrepreneur. We believe it is simply to create something that wasn't there previously, in terms of business achievement that moves you closer to your Future State.

Now this may shock and amaze you, but creation is not a new concept!

Homo sapiens have been inventing and innovating since the dawn of time. If we didn't all possess an inherent capability to be enterprising, the human race would have become extinct thousands of years ago.

The modern author and business guru hasn't invented a new way of performing the act of business, they have merely recoded it and claimed it as their own. We're not going to do that.

Instead we are going to do the opposite, because the act of enterprise is not a novel concept owned by individuals. It's already inside you and the capability to be enterprising is in reach of us all.

We will remind you how by using a simple approach, one that can be used to self-regulate, helping you remain in an optimal enterprise state as long as possible.

The Eight Proverbs

"A short popular saying, usually of ancient origin, that expresses effectively some commonplace truth."

www.dictionary.com, 2015

The Pareto Principle comes into play again. What are the 20% of mindsets that generate 80% of the impact as an entrepreneur?

Faced with the challenge of trying to make sense of working with thousands of entrepreneurs, we turned to the Oxford Dictionary of Proverbs. Why? Because proverbs have passed the test of time and those laws have withstood challenge for hundreds of years. If these sayings did not ring true they would have long been discarded.

In addition, proverbs are simple to understand and easy to remember for any business leader.

Most importantly though, we use proverbs because there can be no better proof that entrepreneurial thinking is not a new discipline. So that seemed a good place to start representing the eight vital enterprise states.

We read all 1,100 proverbs from A to Z before selecting the top 100 that best represent enterprise thinking, in our view. We rationalised that list to 25 laws before finally forcing ourselves to select the top 8, those sayings that best capture how the most effective entrepreneurs think.

MINDSET A: "Why buy a cow when milk is so cheap?"

 OUTSOURCE

The successful entrepreneur is always seeking to raise profit margins by collaborating and engaging external subcontractors and suppliers. When achieved successfully, outsourcing reduces cost, adds in flexibility and removes physical ceilings on production.

To maintain an OUTSOURCING mindset you must be outward looking, unemotional and avoid becoming defensive.

MINDSET B: "If you don't speculate you can't accumulate."

RISK

Whilst this statement may seem obvious, genetically we are programmed for flight, not fight. It's less risky and improves our chance of survival. We have empathy with that reaction, but in business an aversion to risk becomes a limiting factor in that it restricts how far you can take the business. However, you must make sure the risk is calculated, not just blind faith.

To maintain a RISK-focused mindset you must be alert, fearless, confident, unemotional and rational.

MINDSET C: "The worth of a thing is what it will bring."

VALUE

You cannot be in an optimal enterprise state if you underestimate your value.

Be aware of the competition but always price your products and services based on customers' perceived value, not what you think they are worth. That's not your decision.

To maintain a VALUE-focused mindset you must remain open to customer opinion, be constantly listening and bold enough to act.

MINDSET D: "A chain is no stronger than its weakest link."

SKILLS

The act of business is only as good as the people who participate in it. You should constantly be reviewing and testing the capability of your most valuable asset – the people who work with and for you.

Constantly investing in your people is a necessity to realise a Future State.

To maintain a SKILLS-focused mindset you must be constantly seeking out development opportunities and be aware of skills gaps.

MINDSET E: "Success has many fathers, but failure is an orphan."

TEAM

In a traditional sense this proverb rings true i.e., people are quick to claim credit and slow to acknowledge failure. However, in enterprise, it serves as a reminder that success is far more likely if you engage those around you and build effective teams through collaboration.

To maintain a TEAM-focused mindset you must remain supportive not critical, constantly on the lookout for new potential in teams.

MINDSET F: "Why keep a dog and bark yourself?"

DELEGATE

The most precious commodity to an entrepreneur is time. Therefore, the biggest threat is stress and a muddled mind.

While you may be able to do a job and want to control the outcome, failure to delegate limits your potential and hinders your journey to the future state. To maintain a DELEGATE-focused mindset you must be self-aware, buy into 'good enough' and accept people make mistakes as they learn.

MINDSET G: "Four eyes see more than two."

PERSPECTIVE

Decision-making is inherently risky and has the potential to cause costly errors, sometimes business ending. Trusting your instincts is imperative to be successful but you are just *one* set of eyes.

Constantly seeking external opinion challenges thinking and reduces error.

To maintain a PERSPECTIVE-focused mindset you must invite and embrace criticism, making the *big* decisions only after seeking counsel.

MINDSET H: "He who wills the end wills the means."

PLAN (direction)

You must always maintain focus on your Future State and the direction you are heading.

This is not business planning. It is a blueprint against which you test all your actions and ideas.

If an action doesn't accelerate your journey, why do it?

Stop, think, realign.

To maintain a PLAN-focused mindset you must live the Future State, always aware of the bigger picture and resisting tactical urges.

Sounds too easy?

If someone walked into your room right now and slammed their fist on your desk, your ability to remain in an Enterprise State is immediately impacted because you will have an emotional reaction. You can't prevent that, you're only human and it's a natural reaction.

Every day, the human mind must contend with over 35,000 decisions. As a business leader you face a daily storm of challenges to your enterprise state. That's what being an entrepreneur is about, making decisions.

Therefore, the only way to counter attacks on your Enterprise State is to remain acutely aware of your own mindset. That way you can make adjustments as necessary, self-regulating to ensure that even when faced with the most challenging emotional situations, there is a benchmark to return to when the dust settles. Don't try and fight it, accept it. You can't stop yourself from reacting as you are only human, but you can know yourself sufficiently well to realise when you are not in the optimal

Enterprise State. Take control and do something to correct these anomalies.

As you can see, an Enterprise State is far from being a static state of mind. In the real world, you don't adopt a way of thinking for a week, a day, or even a second. The environment around you is constantly changing and the number of inputs to your mind is mind-boggling.

The effect is at best a vibration, at worst an earthquake. You unconsciously make less than optimal decisions because of anger, fear, grief, anxiety, irritation, panic, pity and unhappiness. These are the emotions that have no place in an Enterprise State.

You need to know yourself so that you can return to a centre point, realizing rapidly when life has caused you to go on tilt as an entrepreneur.

The uncomfortable truth for anyone in business is that *personal* challenges remain the biggest barrier to your success. How well you manage these events (attacks on your enterprise mindset) will ultimately determine the level of your performance as an entrepreneur.

We must work tirelessly as entrepreneurs to invest our energies equally in each of the mindsets, always striving to create the perfect Enterprise State. Not today or tomorrow; all the time.

Failure to maintain an Enterprise State, that entrepreneurial mindset, we believe that is why 55% of organisations fail within five years.

It's not the nuts and bolts knowledge you should be worried about. You must know yourself in every moment.

Failure to do so jeopardises your Future State.

know yourself.

Aim too high – overstretch and avoidable risk

Aim too low – fail to realise your potential

No aim at all – strategic drift and waste

KEEP IT SIMPLE TO SUCCEED

CHECK YOUR ENTERPRISE STATE

Please read the following 8 scenarios and answer the questions using the scale of 1 (never) to 10 (definitely)...

A: Thanks to your excellent sales and marketing you have a won a new contract. Your business can just about handle the new workload and it's a great opportunity for the business.

Would you subcontract this work to another business?

B: Your business is growing, but financing production has caused temporary cash flow issues. You are approached by a supplier letting you know a respectable competitor is up for sale at a fair price.

Do you take steps to try and purchase this company?

C: You are completing your annual price review. It's been a great year but a handful of customers have suggested these are hard times. Your competitors have put their prices down recently.

Would you put your prices up?

D: The business has been making the same product for years. Currently, there aren't any complaints. Your employees seem happy and perform well. You are making money. You are contacted by a trainer.

Would you spend money on motivational training for all your staff?

E: You have a critical delivery deadline to hit for one of your main customers. It's slightly behind schedule, though the team are working hard to make it happen.

Would you ignore the situation at this stage?

F: You are booked to present an important seminar to prospective customers. A colleague has asked to go in your place and they seem keen to impress.

Would you arrange for this person to attend in your place?

G: Business is right on track. Everything seems to be working and the income is pouring in. There are a few challenges on the horizon but nothing you can't handle. It's a really busy time for you.

Would you agree to meet a new business consultant?

H: Your business has grown to the point where it is today. You have recently been to a bank seminar advocating that every organisation must have a written business plan to succeed.

Would you agree that a written plan is a "must have"?

Plot your eight answers on the following spider diagram and join the dots.

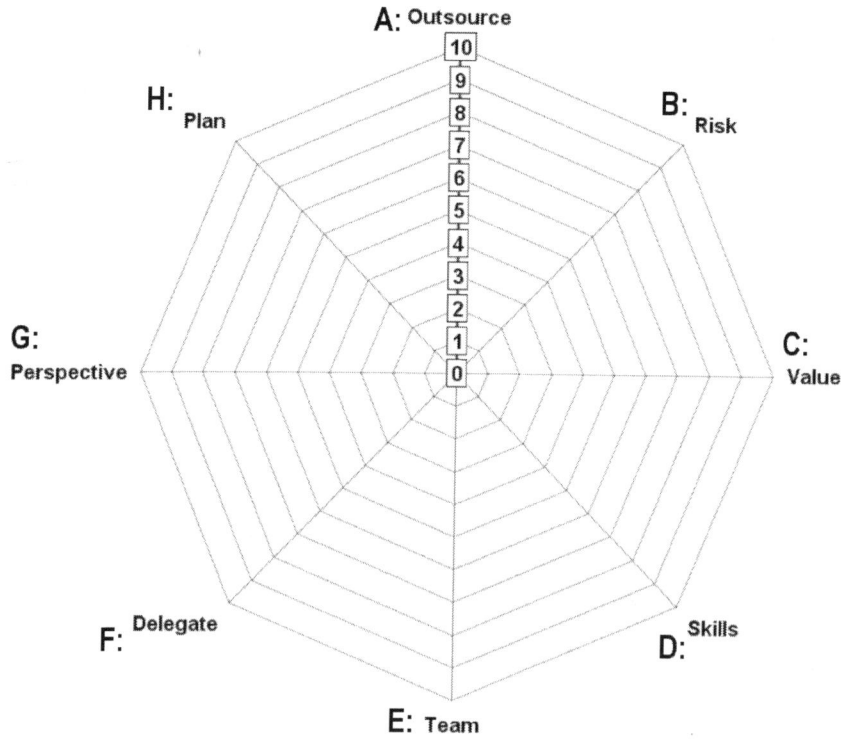

You are now looking at a visual representation of your Enterprise State of mind at this precise moment. You know yourself.

Remember that mindsets are not static and constantly shift. These changes can be rapid as we react to the events around us.

Alternatively, states of mind can be more entrenched (or slow changing) due to our level of attainment in life and business. Both of these factors influence our capability to maintain an optimal Enterprise State and perform the act of business.

To realise a Future State you must remain aware how your environment impacts on your thinking, so you can compensate. Initially, we recommend using the eight proverbs to test your mindset.

Over time, this thinking will become instinctive.

Please note: this exercise is intended purely to embed the eight proverbs. There are no right or wrong answers!

To draw a perfect octagon (no one has ever scored all tens on the Game Change program) is a dangerous place to be as an entrepreneur. We all need at least a modicum of control!

ACT 2: INJECT POWER

Chapter 6
Core Contributors

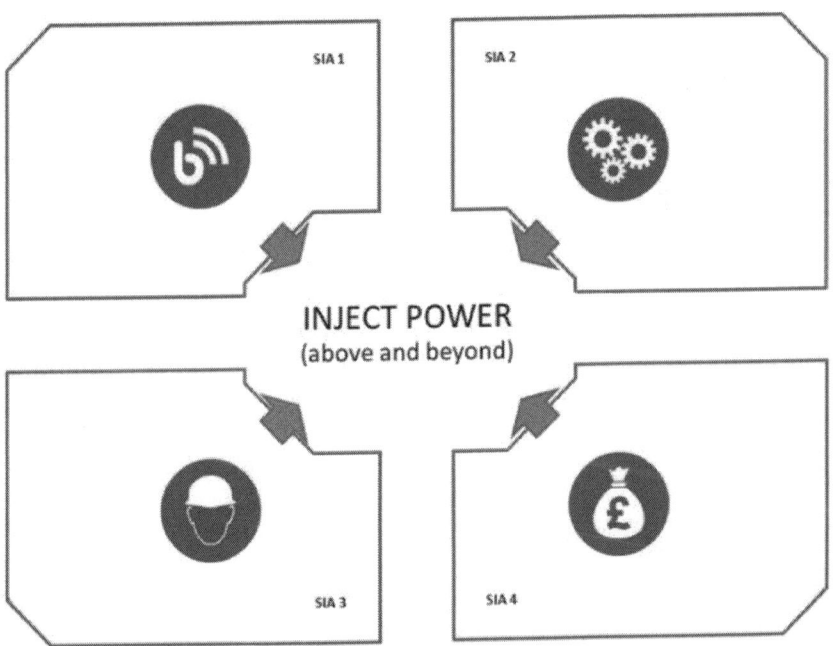

You have now defined a future statement and considered the challenges you need to overcome to remain in an Enterprise State.

Using a self-regulating approach ensures you repeatedly evaluate your performance based on smart, not sweat.

Your future statement may change at some point but not for a while, because your defined destination is based on what you want your perfect existence to be. That ideal doesn't tend to change frequently. Therefore, in our experience, a slight revision is usually only required once every two years or so. Now it's time to inject power into your journey by deciding the critical acts of business needed to translate what is essentially an aspiration into reality.

We have already highlighted the Core Contributors where your energy should be focused, i.e., boosting brand building through marketing and sales, processes, the management of people and finance.

When you isolate the four core contributors to reaching your Future State, the pressure points that generate most impact, then that enables you to invest constantly in these aspects of your business. You become the catalyst for the 20% of action that generates 80% of the business impact.

If you do these aspects of business brilliantly and consistently, performance rapidly improves. If you fail to achieve this level of focus, then the Pareto Principle works in reverse. You find yourself investing the same effort evenly across your organization, frustrated that 80% of your energy is generating just a 20% result.

Or to put it more simply, you and I have the same number of hours in the day; if I spend my day focused on improving high impact activity, you and I shed the same amount of sweat but my results generate four times the results. Every day. You never catch up. THAT is competitiveness.

The Future State Template

We have been very clear that we will not reinvent the wheel in this book. The driving force behind this book is to demonstrate that you can keep it simple, choose what works best for you and reject complexity. We apply the same approach to strategically important action (SIA), the Core Contributors.

We will share with you the 20% of strategies that generate 80% of the impact in:

- Brand/Sales - marketing
- Process
- People
- Money

It's not an exhaustive list, rather it is a summary of the actions we have witnessed work best. When it comes to injecting power into your business performance, you must always keep it simple to succeed.

Selling Out

Let's return to P.T. Barnum for a moment and his belief that it is vital that entrepreneurs retain their integrity. Remember his statement that integrity is 'more precious than diamonds'? These words came from a showman, a circus man and a person some would say was not best placed to start talking about integrity. However, that is the point. Barnum is talking about selling out your *own* personal values for financial gain. There is no one set of values that we must all aspire to.

What integrity means to you may be very different to what it means to someone else, because we all possess a unique set of values which change only marginally throughout our life (usually only when we experience an extreme positive or negative life event). As a result, we all possess a different set of boundaries that dictate what we are prepared to do (and not do) in business to make our Future State a reality.

Before we talk about building brand power, let's clarify what we mean by *brand*. In our experience, people are not always clear what brand actually means. There are two elements: your *brand name* (including your logo, if you have one) and your brand itself. Your 'brand name' exists objectively; people can see it. It's fixed. Your 'brand', by contrast, exists only in someone's mind; it's subjective. Your 'brand name' exists to evoke in the viewer all those things that your brand says about you, without you having to spell it out every time.

When we talk of brand, it is not in terms of your brand name or a superficial list of customer service promises. It is much bigger than that. Your brand is a manifestation of what you believe and stand for in life. In this respect the business and you cannot be separate. For example, you can't lead a business that is democratic and be a despot at heart. Similarly, you can't lead a ruthless performance management set up if you're into peace and love. It doesn't work because authenticity is brand power.

How many times have you come across an organisation whose 'brand message' tries to persuade you to think one thing, but your experience of their service or product leads you to realise that their true brand is something else entirely?

We've all got direct experience of employers who display values and vision statements on the office wall and tell us that's what we should be thinking. You can't dictate how someone else should feel and think because they have to believe in the value before it starts to influence their behaviour.

The same law applies to customers. If you shout that you love the environment but at the same time you sell toxic products, it will be hard to take you seriously. People do try of course. Think of any car manufacturer or petrol company. There's even a specific term for this example - 'green washing'.

Not only is trying to contrive a brand or manipulate its message cynical, it is, ultimately, one of the most damaging things you can do to your business. You will get away with it for a while, but eventually people will see through your attempts and any trust you may have built up over the years will be gone in an instant.

"If I don't get a raise soon, I'm gonna blow the lid off this crummy zoo."

People aren't stupid. Consumers want to feel something when they buy your product. They want an emotional connection with you– that's brand, not a logo and some clever wording.

You need to feel something as well.

You really do need to live and love your brand.

Authenticity is the fuel that builds brand power.

Building Brand Power

At least one of your four strategically important actions on the Future State template must build brand power because that is how you make more profit for doing the same work, that is how you make it harder for competitors to attack and that is what makes it easier to grow sales.

In addition, if your Future State depends on a business sale at the end, a brand building strategy is even more critical as a strong brand will be a key factor in how much your buyer is prepared to pay.

If you are a business that sells to other businesses, rather than directly to the public, then building brand power is still critical. Brand isn't how organisations perceive you because organisations don't perceive anything. It's people within them that do that. In fact, the whole concept of business-to-business 'relationships' is flawed as those relationships and their robustness are based on law not love - contracts not brand.

Your brand power is absorbed by individuals – people - not corporations. It is determined by the strength of the psychological contract that exists between customers, suppliers, staff, employees and you, an agreement that exists but is not written down, tangible or enforceable. However, be in no doubt that this emotional transaction exists.

So how do you build the power of your brand?

You need to keep firmly in mind that brand is how your prospective customers, the markets with whom you intend to communicate, perceive you. Not the other way round. Is it your job to say: "Hmm, let's imagine my customer? What message shall I broadcast to make them buy from me?" Clearly not, as being authentic is a key determinant of brand power.

The worst thing you could do is contrive something because that's what you think your customers want to hear. But you have to say something, so what is it?

Your message will convey four things:

- Your values: the timeless guiding principles that you apply to your business and the way you live.

- Your rules: these are the principles which govern the way you and your business will conduct yourselves.

- The purpose of your business. Why your business exists; a mix of factual and emotional reasons.

- What you do that's valuable to your customers, or to put it another way, how you add value for them. Whatever it is, you need to be able to tell your customers.

There are always going to be people in your chosen markets that don't like the specifics of your product or service, or simply don't like what you stand for. Your job is not to manipulate the message to try and get them to give you the thumbs up. Don't waste your valuable time knocking on a door that is difficult to open. Rather use your time to communicate your brand to the people who, when they hear your message, will say: "Hey, I like what they are saying. I want to be part of their tribe".

Be utterly paranoid about protecting your brand. Be single-minded in making sure nothing happens to damage it. Even if you think you don't have a brand, you do. You can't stop people deciding for themselves what your brand promises. The only difference, in this scenario, is you aren't doing anything to protect and nurture it!

Brand building strategies need to constantly build capability in delivering an experience that *exceeds* your customer promise and values, every time. Your reputation and Future State depend on it.

The Fallacy of Competitive Advantage

Let's consider examples of accepted thinking on building competitive advantage, or put more simply, how to be better than competitors.

- Strong research and innovation
- High volume production
- Access to working capital
- Levels of customer support
- Distribution rights
- Better equipment (capital assets)
- Flexibility
- Efficiency
- Lower pricing

The list goes on and there's an extensive library of books on Amazon dedicated to all these topics. However, after working directly with organisations and always being challenged to improve performance against competitors, we can say with some confidence that the only competitive advantage that cannot be copied (with time and money) is your brand.

Brand strength is the strongest defence against attack, stopping competitors taking your customers because they are loyal to your business. It is the fastest way to win a larger share of the market, taking your competitors' customers by clearly articulating what your business is all about and, most importantly, how you will provide something that is more valuable to them. This is your 'brand promise'.

Once you have an inherent understanding of your brand promise, write it down. That's the only way you can know when you fail to live up to that promise. Only then can you take corrective action before finding your name blackened all over social media.

Just Words: Barclays Banking Group

"We create a diverse and inclusive environment where colleagues can fulfil their potential. We positively impact on the communities in which we operate. We act with integrity in everything we do. We create sustainable returns above the cost of equity."

Source: www.home.barclays/about-barclays/balanced-scorecard. December, 2015

That's how Barclays want you to see and feel their brand, the benchmark they have bought into. Whether they actually live up to that promise in all their actions is another story and ultimately for you decide. However, any failure to do so at any given moment in time creates brand damage.

On a micro level, I recently met a woman who works for Barclays and was angry with her employer because her manager is dictatorial. That's just one person's story and there are always two sides to every story. However, that is still brand damage, because people talk.

That woman felt moved to criticise, because in her eyes, the explicit brand promise made by Barclays did not translate into her actual experience. This disjoint generates negative emotions and, if unchecked, that frustration and disappointment spill over into criticising the business.

Be very careful what you write down as your brand values, as your role is to ensure they are a reality.

To provide some balance, the person also told me that the bank frequently donates money to local schools and groups. That's brand building as it meets their promise. Experiences change how potential customers feel about your brand and their propensity to buy into it.

Too Short: Nike

"To bring inspiration and innovation to every athlete. If you have a body you are an athlete."

Source: http://about.nike.com. December, 2015

Using a little artistic interpretation, we assume they mean everything Nike does must be innovative and designed to inspire customers i.e., Nike respects everyone interested in sport, whatever their capabilities.

Simple is good, but the fact I had to use my imagination isn't a positive.

Two lines isn't enough because it leaves too much space for interpretation.

These words are actually a slogan and not a brand promise. It is difficult to know where to invest in building brand power if it has no substance.

You build brand power by creating the capability to meet and preferably exceed, your promises. That means you must constantly invest in better skills, people and process.

Most importantly, it demands an ability to recognise immediately when your business has broken a promise and rapidly fix it. Not when an unhappy customer calls and complains, that's too late, the damage is done (think how many don't bother to call).

Your written brand promise is the mirror that enables you to judge your own actions and make adjustments before standards slip. In business, compared with brand, there is nothing else that holds as much potential to make your business a success or ruin it - in equal measure.

Going Knievel

Evel Knievel is the infamous daredevil motorcyclist from the seventies. He was a troubled character, in reality, and far from a role model. However, there has been no one else in history as committed to living their brand.

In 1975, he was booked to do a motorcycle jump over thirteen buses at the old Wembley Stadium in the UK. It was his debut in the country but with a few weeks to go, he was shocked to discover only 7000 of the 90000 tickets had been sold. He realised that the brand 'Evel Knievel' had no power in the UK, as people didn't know who he was or what he stood for.

In an act of desperation, Knievel decided to draw as much attention to himself as possible by doing audacious acts in the run up to the show. He started by driving his custom Cadillac car around the London Circular on the wrong side of the road, causing traffic chaos because according to him: 'you Brits drive on the wrong side'. Knievel continued to deliver a series of promotional stunts, actions and words that reflected his brand promise - that on that day at Wembley he would be daring, dangerous and exciting. In just a few short weeks the stadium was a complete sell-out.

During the campaign Knievel had repeatedly promised the public that he would clear thirteen buses. However, the day before the jump Knievel inspected the ramp that had been specially constructed for his leap. It was at this moment he realised that, even though Wembley was the UK's largest arena, there just wasn't enough distance to reach the speed needed to clear all thirteen vehicles. A bystander heard Knievel talking to himself: "Hell, I can't do that, I can't jump that far".

Knievel was going to crash. The team around him suggested removing a bus but he refused outright, adamant that the leap had to go ahead unchanged.

"I said I'd jump thirteen". What happened next cannot be described any more perfectly than the passage from Stuart Barker's book Life of Evel:

"On the day of the jump, Evel came storming down the flimsy, narrow ski ramp at about 80 mph, raised his body slightly off his Harley and took off smoothly to rapturous applause. The jump was long and narrow and looked to be going well, but his analysis proved accurate and Knievel landed roughly and slightly sideways on the thirteenth bus.

Evel was thrown high in the air, almost performing a handstand while still desperately struggling to hold onto the Harley's handlebars, and as the bike bucked and tossed at high speed, Knievel was finally forced to let go and his body slammed into the Wembley turf, where he rolled end over end, churning up the dust.

The rogue bike eventually caught up with him and slammed him hard in front of a terrified and silenced audience. Knievel fractured vertebrae, broke his pelvis, his right hand and one finger.

Yet with pure Knievel bravado, still pumped full of adrenalin and in too much shock to feel just how bad his injuries were, Evel asked to address the crowd, to wild applause.

As he collapsed and was rushed to hospital he turned to his promoter and apologized, saying: "My Grandma always taught me to catch the last bus".

Years later Knievel was asked why he went ahead with the jump when he knew the crash was inevitable.

"In the end we knew we couldn't get the right gearing for the Harley in time, so we just had to go ahead with the jump... *the crowd had paid their money.*"

That's what Knievel was prepared to do for his brand, to risk his life to keep his promise and own personal integrity.

In a single year in the seventies, his branded toys earned him $20 million. That was the brand power he had built in business, through living his values every day and being true to himself.

What would you do for your brand?

The answer should be whatever it takes – but maybe let's draw the line at risking our lives. We can't all be Evel Knievel!

KEEP IT SIMPLE TO SUCCEED

Write down:

- The values that guide you in your life and in business.

- The rules that govern the way you and your business will conduct yourselves. What you are you prepared to do, and what are you not prepared to do?

- What emotions will your customers experience? Will they feel happy? Secure? Educated?

- What you do that is valuable to your customers? How you add value for them?

This list is the essence of your brand. In fact, it is your brand.

It will act as your moral compass. It will be the foundation of every business decision you make. There may be easier paths in business but if they don't fit in with your values and brand then you turn away, as there will be a price to pay later, emotionally and financially, as your brand will become damaged.

When it comes to building brand power you are creating an emotional bond with your customers and prospective customers that makes them want to be part of your tribe.

A psychological contract is being formed, where in return for them parting with their money, you make a promise that they know they can trust you to keep.

That is brand power. You have authenticity and integrity and the customer can trust you to deliver what you promise, every time. Because you have created a stronger bond with your customers through this promise, they are prepared to pay you a premium for your product or service compared to your less trusted competitor.

Be continuously and acutely aware:

- When it comes to integrity one size does not fit all - always do what's right for you.

- Live your values and avoid culture shock - promising one thing, delivering another.

- Nurture people to adopt your brand values in a way that suits them, don't dictate.

- Never compromise your brand promise for profit - customers will see right through you in time.

- LOVE your brand (and business).

Remember that when your journey ends and you arrive at your Future State, you will need a degree of 'corporate karma' to sleep at night.

Chapter 7
Above and Beyond: Marketing

Now it's time to isolate your game changing strategies because you can only inject power if you know how you will arrive at the Future State. Otherwise, your energy is spread thinly and randomly.

When we talk of core contributors it is critical that an ABOVE and BEYOND approach is applied to marketing and sales, operations, people and money. It is not going to be enough to create and implement these strategies 'quite well', it has to be done brilliantly, constantly improving and never accepting the 'good enough' principle in these four critical areas. We can accept that for the thousands of other contributory actions in your business, but not the core.

In this way you will be living the Pareto Principle and your business progress will be exponential.

"You must be careful that your goods are valuable; that they are genuine, and will give satisfaction. When you get an article which you know is going to please your customers, and that when they have tried it, they will feel they have got their money's worth, then let the fact be known that you have got it. Now I don't say that everybody should advertise, but I say if you have got goods for sale, and you don't, the chances are that someday the sheriff will do it for you. It is obvious, you must be known in some way, else how could you be supported?"

Advertise Your Business. Golden Rules for Making Money. P.T. Barnum (1880).

Never forget that while people, money, and processes are vital for any business, there is no need for any of those functions if you have no customers. It's not necessary to become a marketing expert to win new business. However, to create effective strategies, you must be able to recognise the opportunities.

You can do that two ways, instinctively (high-risk, short-term, low gain) or using principles that have been in existence since Shakespeare's time in The Merchant of Venice.

As we've said before, our goal is not to reinvent the wheel and regurgitate it as our own, it is to strip down the mass of marketing theory and highlight the 20% of strategies that generate 80% of the impact, not in theory, but in practice - to keep it simple to succeed.

Revisiting the Product Life Cycle

Just as there is a business life cycle, your products and services follow a similar trajectory. Everything declines to death if you keep doing the same thing.

All products and services have a start-up phase where demand is unproven. If customers want a product, it increases in popularity and revenue increases steeply. The product or service then matures as competitors launch substitute alternatives and supply increases. The number of people who want the product naturally diminishes (they already have it or better alternatives are being launched).

Revenue now plateaus because prices stagnate or decline as competitors try to secure a diminishing number of sales opportunities. You are forced to react in kind.

Finally, there is a decline to death as profit margins are squeezed so much that eventually it is no longer economically viable to sell the product or service.

Once again, this is not a maybe, it will happen to every product and service in your range unless you create a new curve by innovating and adapting the offer. Products and services are constantly being reinvented in a bid to extend their life. Your role is to optimise the profit generated throughout this cycle.

If it's Not Broken: The Boston Matrix

To realise your Future State, you must know the right time to invest in strategies, creating new products and services that will take you to that destination. There have been many studies on this aspect of marketing, the most famous and best is still the Boston Matrix, or Boston Box, developed by Boston Consulting Group (BCG) in the seventies

By *marrying* the Boston Matrix to the Product Life Cycle, it becomes a practical decision-making tool for entrepreneurs rather than an academic exercise.

A) START-UP: Question marks

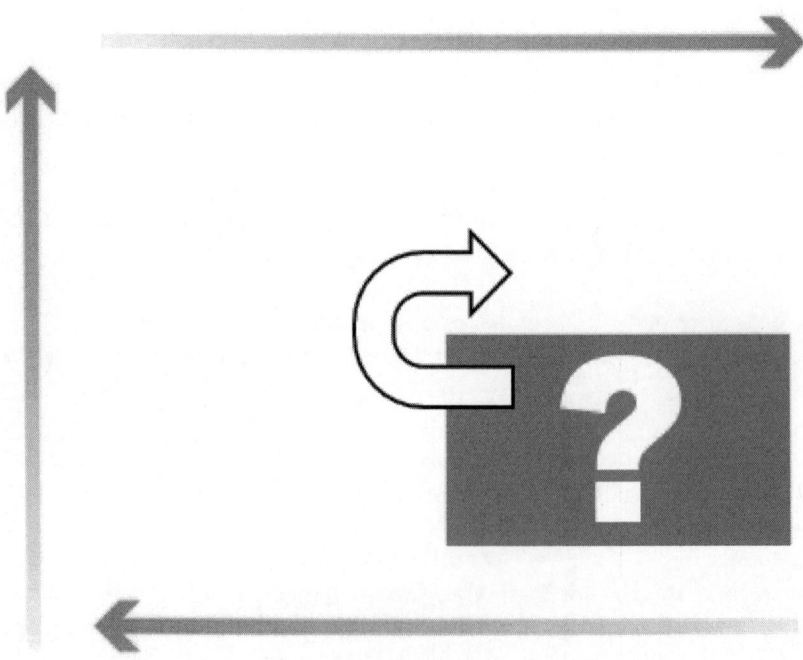

If you are in the services sector you can often create a new 'product' with just a pad and a pen. However, if you are in physical product development, this process can be extremely expensive and time-consuming.

Either way, you should always be thinking of the next potential star offering for your business.

If you create and sell physical products, then it is likely the research and development process will be one of your core contributors. Market readiness must be achieved rapidly and economically to compete.

A business cannot afford to create too many question mark products that fail to become stars. If you do that too many times, you go out of business, as revenue is insufficient to cover your investments in the long term. You can't afford to just be 'good enough' at this process, as performance has to be ABOVE and BEYOND what is the norm in your industry.

Similarly, if you are fortunate enough to be in the services sector or the knowledge economy selling advice, whilst you may not have the challenge of creating tangible products that are in demand, your work on branding and processes must be above and beyond.

If you create too many question mark services that fail to become stars your existing offering declines to death.

Whilst it can be extremely challenging to keep thinking of the next best thing when you are struggling or profiting in the moment, it is strategically important that you do so, because you now know that *the Future State depends on it.*

B) GROWTH: Stars

If you have a product or service with sales momentum, during this growth phase you must have a strategy to ensure profit-margins are optimised and to maintain your brand promise while meeting that demand.

During the growth period, your competitors are struggling to catch up and these products and services generate maximum profit margin.

However, it is still vital that you continue to invest in the next best thing. That may mean funding a sales and marketing campaign, investing the profits generated back into those high potential products and services, because you know that you must continue to speculate to accumulate.

C) MATURITY TO DECLINE: Cash Cows

When your products and services start levelling off in sales growth, they are generating maximum profit because you no longer need to invest large sums to support them. Everything is already in place to deliver.

Your strategies at this stage will probably involve market research and adaptation to extend the life of this previously star offering or product (the profit period). You implement tweaks, focusing on evolution not revolution. However, you know the final phase is inevitable ... decline to death.

Price competition is looming on the horizon.

D) DEATH: Dogs

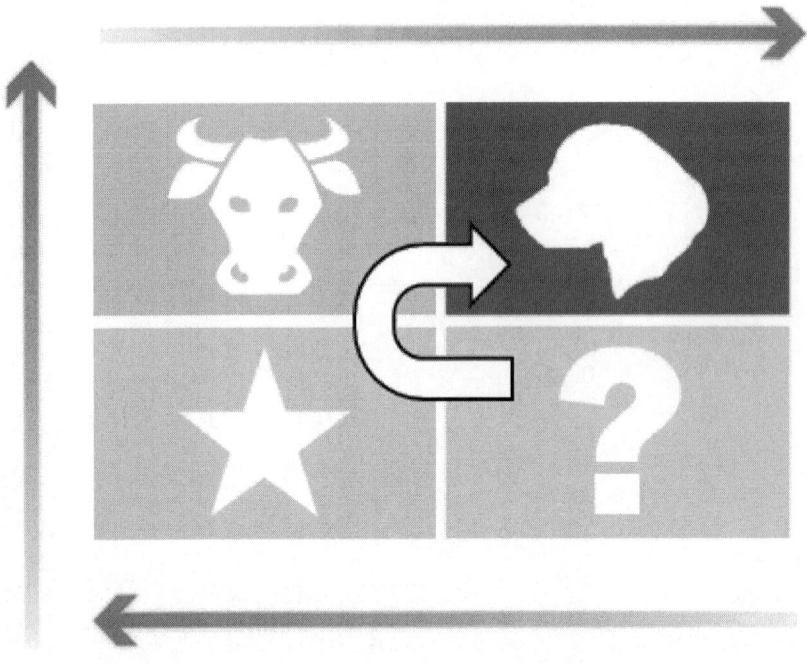

The market is now saturated with competitors and the number of potential customers is rapidly declining.

It is critical that you realise when you are investing in the inevitable decline to death phase, because that is effectively throwing good money after bad.

There is a significant opportunity cost to your business of failing to recognise this effect in a timely manner, because every pound and minute you spend propping up a dying product or service could have been invested in the next question mark.

That investment could have been redirected to boost the next potential star offering, one that could transform your business future and accelerate your business along the path to the Future State.

Four Strategies

The second essential marketing chart and concept you need to understand is based on the Ansoff Matrix. Once again, this is a consultancy driven model, so we should inject some reality and simplicity into the theory

Every business should have a minimum of four marketing strategies running at any one time. At least one of these marketing strategies will be strategically important to realising your Future State.

Your challenge is to decide which one needs the most significant ABOVE and BEYOND investment.

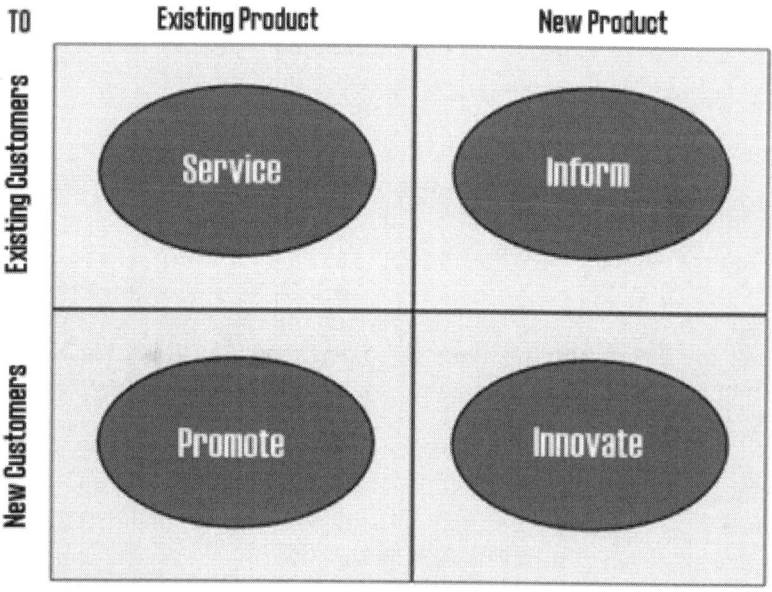

PRIORITY 1:
Sell EXISTING product (service) to EXISTING customers (current/past)

This scenario is always our favourite marketing option because it is the cheapest, fastest and the easiest to execute.

If you need to generate cash quickly this has to be the primary source because you don't have to sell your brand – the targets have already bought into your values and trust you to deliver.

In terms of sales, persuading people to trust you is at least two-thirds of the challenge and effort. In the case of past and existing customers, assuming you delivered your brand promise effectively and at least met expectations, these people already have a positive experience using your brand. As a result, there is no doubt in their minds, they buy without question and become powerful advocates - they tell all their friends.

SERVICE strategies stimulate a positive reaction in existing customers and require above and beyond communication - at frequent and regular intervals.

Day-to-day living is a frenetic process for all of us. Typically, people don't fail to repeat purchase because they dislike your business (assuming you did a good job). They don't buy from you again because they've forgotten. Your brand awareness has fallen out of their consciousness. Your brand strength is dormant within them because that past experience is logged in their memory, but to download it you need to 'hit the right button'. In marketing terms that might mean social media updates, email communication, offers i.e., anything planned that causes past and existing customers to think of your brand again.

To illustrate how powerful the act of communicating with existing customers can be, a few years ago we worked with a food manufacturer who refused to send out customer updates because he was adamant they did not want to be bothered and would react negatively.

When analysing his sales figures we noticed a spike in unit sales every January. The business leader had failed to make the link that the start of the year is when he sends out his annual price-rise notice. Let's pause and reflect on this experience for a moment. No one likes to hear the prices of their purchases are going up. It's probably one of the most challenging messages for a business to deliver successfully. This business wasn't sending out a positive sales and marketing message, he was sending out the worst kind of news for customers: your costs are going up. Yet the unit sales still spiked.

In reality, the mere act of communication had stimulated demand, because his past customers had forgotten his brand. They heard from the business so infrequently that awareness had weakened over time. That annual price increase letter was a reminder, even though that wasn't the intention of the communication. The contact alone was enough to stimulate increased orders because it was a catalyst, causing past customers to relive their brand experience and want to repeat it.

If you complete a proactive action in business there will always be a reaction. You influence whether that response is positive or negative.

That relationship is a certainty in marketing and life.

PRIORITY 2:
Sell NEW product (service) to EXISTING customers (current/past)

This is our second favourite marketing strategy because once again you don't have to invest two-thirds of your energy in persuading customers your brand is credible. Strategies to increase sales of new products to existing customers are inform-based. You must put in place a communication strategy to regularly inform this group of any new products and services. Customers cannot be expected to purchase your new products if you don't tell them they exist!

We appreciate there's a balance between helpful updates and intrusive contact and you will need to decide what that balance is, after speaking to a sample of customers. However, assuming you delivered on your brand promise previously, past and existing customers will listen to your recommendations and will try a new option because they trust you. When you vouch for something, you must keep delivering on your promise. Any new offer must be bullet-proof. Otherwise, that trust is lost and it becomes difficult and costly to recapture.

INFORM strategies stimulate new product sales and can be a rapid and reliable source of revenue. Existing and past customers are the least painful source of the working capital needed to grow an organisation i.e., the money needed to finance the act of business.

PRIORITY 3:
Sell EXISTING product (service) to NEW customers (never bought)

The third strategy you must have in place involves promoting your existing product (service) to new markets, people who have not bought into your brand.

Overcoming this challenge can be hard work and costly, as you now have to spend two-thirds of your energy and effort persuading the customer the business can be trusted in the first place, *plus* still having to sell the advantages of your product and service.

Selling existing products and services to new customers, demands strategies that deliver creative marketing material, effective brand messages (promoting awareness of your brand, not necessarily selling product) and of course, once again, regular communication with the target audiences.

PROMOTIONAL strategies are critical as they generate a new crop of customers, new contacts who then transfer to existing / past status (easier money).

92

You do still have an advantage in this scenario as your existing and past customers can be encouraged to vouch for your brand, through testimonial and case study.

Production of advocate stories is critical, as third party endorsement is essential if customers don't know you.

Without this support you could be anyone!

FINALLY:
Sell NEW products (services) to NEW customers (never bought)

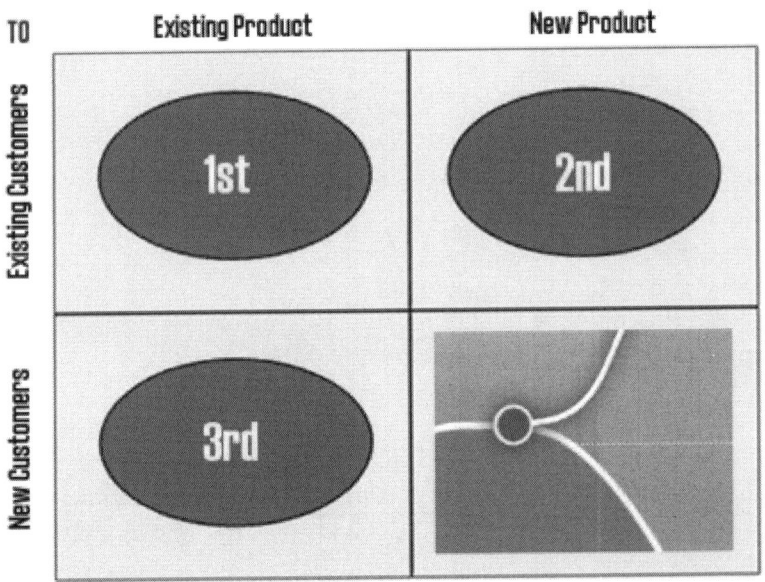

'New to new' is the greatest challenge in marketing and sales.

Revenue is low initially as you must invest in new ideas, implementing INNOVATE strategies to penetrate the new market.

In this scenario, there is no one to vouch for your product (service), the customers you are targeting do not know you and treat your brand promise with suspicion. This demands high levels of marketing activity.

Despite our obvious lack of enthusiasm for this box on the matrix, we know it is also the most important because that is how we create new curves, i.e., constantly developing new products and services for new customers; otherwise, decline to death.

For these reasons every business must be simultaneously implementing at least four marketing strategies because existing customers finance the future, generating the cash and money needed to create new curves.

If you run out of cash - no Future State.

The Most Important Graph in Marketing

The most common mistake entrepreneurs make when creating marketing and sales strategies is to assume they are the customer. They make decisions based on what they think and feel, not their customers' needs and emotions which obviously can be very different.

We recently spoke to the leaders of a white goods retailer who had spent a month deciding what 35-year-old women think and need when selecting a washing machine. Their Board of Directors had an average age of 55 and was exclusively male. That's quite a leap. We recommended throwing out conjecture and replacing that with the opinion of real customers. All they had to do was ask.

If you get this process wrong, you create products and marketing that people don't respond to and don't want. Your products fail at the question mark phase of the product life cycle and cause losses which could have been avoided.

If you make this mistake too many times, your business will fail.

The most important curve in marketing, the standard distribution bell curve, reminds us to market to the 80% not a vocal minority.

That is the difference between high and low sales in business.

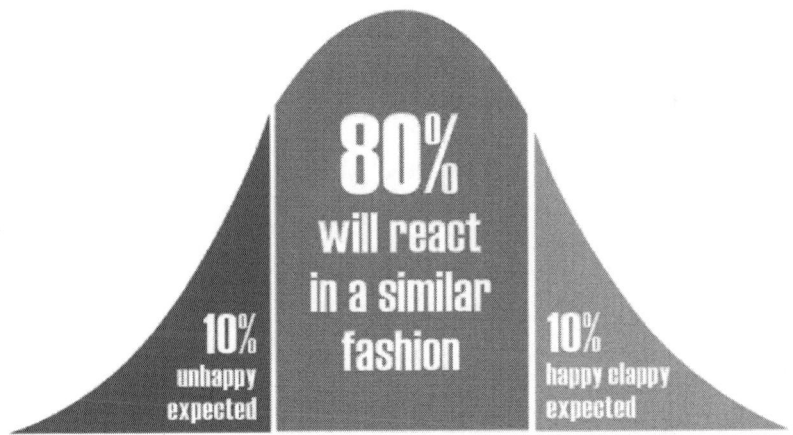

For example, if we line up one hundred people randomly, on average 80 per cent of them will react in a similar fashion to anything we say. Their behaviour has an element of predictably and it is this group we listen to when deciding how to create marketing strategies.

The 20% in the tails of the curve, the minority, they shout loudest and our natural instinct as human beings is to listen to their voices more, because they are more forceful.

But in reality nothing has changed, they remain the minority and their irrational responses teach us little about markets.

Therefore:

REJECT IRRATIONAL HAPPY

We can't explain this phenomenon but in our experience, there are always 10% of customers who are irrationally delighted. They embrace your brand unconditionally. They tell you they love you and when asked to buy into your new ideas they gush with enthusiasm. They promise to buy and believe it wholeheartedly when they say it. There *is* money to be made in this minority group because willing customers make easy brand advocates. However, when deciding marketing strategies, they are extremely dangerous people. Most of your family and friends are in this grouping as it is rare for someone who cares for you to give a rational response, even in the face of reality.

You need to reject these people's opinions and create strategies based on the majority view, feedback founded on fact not fandom.

REJECT IRRATIONAL UNHAPPY

Similarly, there is a minority of people who complain and gripe whatever you do in business. It's inexplicable again, but this 10% of people exist in a negative state and will disagree and doubt, regardless of anything you do or say to change that stance. This is an extremely dangerous group of people when it comes to marketing, because they shout loudest. But their thinking is irrational so how can you make a reliable judgement based on their views?

We are certain that many viable marketing ideas die on desks unnecessarily because entrepreneurs pander to the views of the irrationally unhappy. In fact, we have witnessed businesses fail as a direct result. It's not the entrepreneur's fault, because for decades there have been countless textbooks on service insisting the customer is always right. In the real world that is utter rubbish. In reality the cause of this irrational unhappiness is due to poor marketing performance because anybody who buys your product and behaves this way shouldn't have been a target in the first place. That is why these negative emotional responses manifest. As a result, if we accept these people were never going to engage with our products and services in the first place, their opinions should carry no weight when it comes to creating marketing strategies. Consider their views but dismiss them.

That action doesn't have to be a negative experience. If a customer is not in your target market, decide not to work with them and improve your marketing messages so they know they shouldn't buy your product. That decision should be a positive experience for all parties.

We would certainly never advocate upsetting a customer, but one of the benefits of running your own business is having the freedom to control your own destiny. As we have said previously, the most powerful weapon you have as an entrepreneur is the word 'no'.

Help these people become happier - refer them to a competitor.

A word of caution, though. Don't confuse the irrationally unhappy, with the rationally unhappy. Those people you do have to do something about, and quickly!

When you are creating marketing strategies and new products you must ALWAYS market for the 80% reaction.

KEEP IT SIMPLE TO SUCCEED

STEP 1

EXISTING/NEW products (services) to EXISTING customers

- Define who your high value customers are (targets)
- Write down a list of sales messages
- Schedule a diary of contact

Then make sure you have the resources in place to make it happen.

You must prioritise increasing existing customer spend over the other strategies in the matrix because this easier money helps fund the rest. Financing your campaigns and reaching your Future State will be far more challenging if you fail to do so.

STEP 2:

Identify your four strategies (one for each box in the matrix), new ideas that will better engage new, existing and past customers.

1 SERVICE | 2 INFORM | 3 PROMOTE | 4 INNOVATE

N.B. Your ideas must be above and beyond what you already do in terms of marketing and sales. The ideas must contribute to accelerating your Future State.

Chapter 8
Above and Beyond: Process

When you carefully work out the costs of your products and services and set a price for them that should give you a healthy margin at the end of the year. So why is it that at the end of the year you never seem to have that exact amount of money in the bank?

Profit-margin is not predictable because the actions you take to fulfil orders and complete the act of business do not take place in a controlled environment. Business is dynamic with thousands of simultaneously shifting conditions every day.

How well you manage and control the act of business dictates how accurately your forecasts translate into reality. That is the difference between making a profit or a loss, because no one ever intentionally creates a business plan to lose money and go bust!

You bleed margin during the act of doing business (process).

"A person who does business by rule, having a time and place for everything, will accomplish twice as much and with half the trouble of him who does it carelessly and slipshod. Of course, there is a limit to all these rules. We must try to preserve the happy medium, for there is such a thing as being too systematic. There are men and women, for instance, who put away things so carefully that they can never find them again."

Be Systematic. Golden Rules for Making Money. P.T. Barnum (1880).

Whilst there are literally thousands of systems and processes in play during a typical business day, there are only ever a small number that are *strategically important* and cause exponential impact on performance. That impact can be positive or negative depending on your decisions as a business leader. Once you have identified these strategically important processes, then you can apply the Pareto Principle and invest more energy and resource into the people and tools that complete those vital tasks - ABOVE and BEYOND the level expected in your industry.

Your role as a business leader is to accurately identify where most value is added for customers in the act of business and create strategies to ensure this happens every time. Failure to do so results in avoidable waste (time and material) and inadvertently building cost into a process, not value.

Customers do not pay for waste, you do.

The customer is only willing to pay for value.

Value Mapping

Value mapping is a technique long established in the manufacturing sector but less so in the services industry. However, the methods and principles apply equally in terms of detecting opportunities and identifying threats within your systems and processes.

There is an entire consultancy sector built on process improvement. However, in our view it's just not that complicated and every entrepreneur is capable of using visual mapping to isolate steps in the process that put pressure on profit. These are the pinch points that are highest risk, eroding your margins and opportunity.

As sequences of actions are always linked in a chain, it only takes one mistake or oversight to make an entire process unprofitable.

When you identify these high stress points, strategies can be implemented to improve monitoring and performance at these critical stages in the act of business. Profit seepage is reduced and margin is protected. Your forecast bears a much closer resemblance to reality at the end of the year.

Back to the Drawing Board

The only way to isolate strategically important processes is to *visualise* the ebb and flow of money as it moves through your operation, from the very start to the very end. That means drawing out a process step by step.

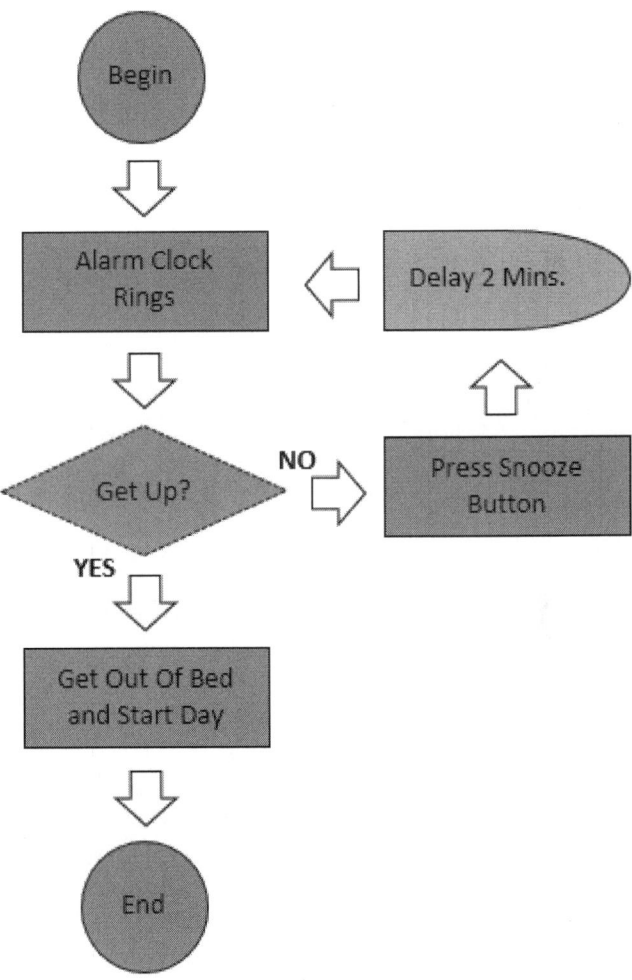

In business, processes actually commence long before a customer places an order. Sales and marketing is a process. Research and development prior to even launching your products and services is a sequence of actions. We increase profit margin by creating repeatable performance in key areas. The actions speed up when people become more familiar with a process; that is *increased productivity*. The other advantage of visual mapping is the opportunity to strip out waste; that is *increased efficiency*.

The most significant ideas for efficiencies and savings will always come from the people working in the process itself, doing the work every day, because they hold the experience needed to recommend improvements. First, always ask your employees how they would improve their own processes – then start your own investigation.

At the risk of sounding amateurish, get yourself a pack of post-its and invite the people involved in your processes into a room. Start sticking the sequence of actions on the wall. That's how paid consultants do it!

You can then rapidly identify patterns and isolate any fracture points in the process, because there will be tangible symptoms in the room, the ones your staff experience first-hand.

Those symptoms may appear as waiting around unnecessarily for others in the process to finish, being forced into rework due to errors, throwing items away because of overproduction or failing to meet quotas on time due to insufficient availability of resources (people, materials).

All of these events generate a negative emotional response in the people working within a process. Hence, you can very quickly identify profit seepage in a process, because the signs manifest physically and your staff will be bursting to tell you about how you can improve their existence!

Any failings in processes are inbuilt and occur every time the tasks are performed. As a result, any profit seepage is part of the DNA of your business model and will be *forever destined to erode your profit* unless you make a change, implementing process improvement. Of course, on the flip side any gains you make in a process will also be repeated every time the process is executed.

Action 1: Eliminate Wasteful Action

Once you have visually mapped out your process, be it marketing or something more tangible such as production, then you need to isolate those elements that add most value and impact on performance exponentially.

Value mapping consultants typically classify each step in a process as follows:

- V = VALUE ADDING – increases the value of the product or service being delivered (in customers' eyes)

- E = ESSENTIAL – these actions are necessary to enable value adding activity, they do not add value in themselves

- N = NON VALUE ADDING – superfluous, unnecessary - why are they happening?

Believe it or not, non-value-adding activities are actually quite common. They occur when people over-engineer and/or over-complicate what they do, usually due to lack of experience.

Non-value-adding steps in a process can also develop organically and may not actually be listed in the approved way of performing activities. This effect occurs because people decide they know best or lack the skills needed to complete the step as designed, in other words they take short cuts.

Value mapping does not measure what we think the process is, it measures the reality. It maps what it is actually occurring whether we like it or not.

Non-value-adding activity wastes energy. It leads to increased delay and higher labour costs. These actions erode margins and reduce competitiveness.

How Does It Work?

When you visually map out the steps in a process you must classify each one as value- adding, essential or non-value-adding.

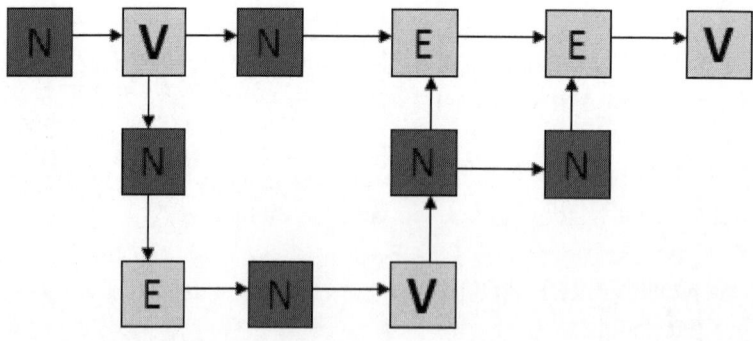

Those steps that add no value and are non-essential should be challenged. Are there better ways of achieving the same outcome?

Do these actions and activities need to be part of the process at all?

If the answer is no, remove them.

After this rationalising you should be able to draw out a much simpler and faster version of the same process – this is what is meant by LEAN.

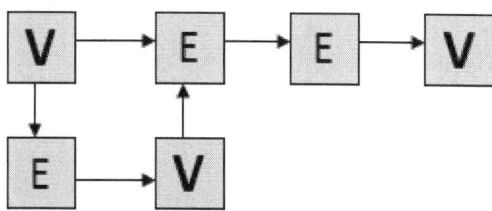

You will then need to create a strategy to transform the old process into the new. The accepted approach to enable process improvement is to create a culture of ongoing checks and controls: Identify, Understand, Eliminate, Dilute and Change.

Any changes to working practice may take time to implement successfully, requiring money and patience while the changes are embedded and behaviour is relearnt, fine tuning as you go. People will have to relearn and own the new process which is why it is always better driven from the bottom, rather than imposed from above. There is no stronger buy-in than people *perceiving* that the changes are driven by their own ideas and suggestions.

People Break Processes

Profit-margin is most commonly eroded in the transition from one step in a process to another. These interfaces, or handover events, should be monitored closely and repeatedly.

In truth, it is usually people that break processes by not following the system, consciously through taking short cuts, or unconsciously because of poor communication. This is where management proves their worth by being aware of what's going on at these high risk interfaces.

You should incorporate strategies to reinforce these weak points and ensure that resources are available to manage the new processes – training, better tools, improved communication and better policing (management).

"I can't move my head."

Never underestimate the importance of rules when it comes to processes and people. People break processes, rules protect them.

Process must be supported by clear systems – written procedures which are designed to manage the processes. The system will set out clearly what is permissible and what is not. Contrary to enterprise, systems are not democratic; we are striving for a 'one best way' solution.

When it comes to strategically important processes, any deficiencies now or in future will compromise your Future State, as you will have less profit for investment and risk breaking your brand promise (delay/errors).

Universal Mapping

Visual mapping is not exclusive to manufacturing. It's a universally valuable tool for every business.

For example, visual mapping is critical in our own business even though we produce no tangible product. One of the most important processes in Business Think is marketing and sales.

To be successful in consultancy demands a constant stream of new prospects to maintain brand awareness (reputation) and generate new sales.

The actions in the marketing and sales process produce no physical outputs in themselves, as it is a knowledge-based system. However, each step is still submitted to value mapping scrutiny and ongoing process improvement.

Any delays in sending out campaigns damage our business on a number of levels. We generate fewer customers (cash and profit), there is an unacceptable break in brand communication with customers (diminished awareness) and we fail to stimulate word of mouth in the market place.

The early challenges with this process were predictably at the interfaces, when people passed on messages or took receipt of information produced earlier. We implemented a strategy to improve quality control and introduced training to ensure less confusion, guaranteeing sales messages were high quality.

Every business leader must implement strategies that simplify and shorten the timeline by *ruthlessly removing* non-value-adding activity. If you have no staff, there is a need to map and analyse your *own* actions.

People break processes. It is vital that the people involved in a process are trained to deliver optimal performance during the value adding activity. These strategies make a business more competitive and accelerate the Future State.

Always remember: Your customers don't pay for waste – you do.

KEEP IT SIMPLE TO SUCCEED

1. Review your Future Statement and Above and Beyond Marketing.

2. Isolate a process that is critical to adding value for the target customers.

3. Observe and draw the steps in that process from start to finish.

4. Invite the people involved in the process to discuss the drawing and suggest revisions (based on their experience); that may be just you!

5. Classify each step as Value-Adding, Essential or Non-Value.

6. Estimate level of risk to profit margins at the interfaces.

7. Suggest improvements.

Your ideas must be ABOVE and BEYOND what you already do in terms of process improvement and must directly contribute to realising your Future State.

Chapter 9
Above and Beyond: People

"Anyone engaging employees should be careful to get the best. Understand, you cannot have too good tools to work with, and there is no tool you should be as particular about as living tools. An important element in an employee is the brain. You can see bills up, 'Hands Wanted', but 'hands' are not worth a great deal without 'heads'."

Use the Best Tools. Golden Rules for Making Money. P.T. Barnum (1880).

When it comes to people, your role is to ensure the business has the right number of people, with the right skills, at the right time, in the right place. You can only know those four measures by using a Future State as the benchmark. If you don't have employees, the goals are the same, albeit your challenge is to influence people outside the business to help you.

It may seem a pretty obvious thing to say, but your people need to be capable of doing their job. What does it mean to be *capable*?

CAPABILITY = CAPACITY + COMPETENCE

Or, in plainer language, you make sure your people have enough time, resources and skills to do the work required, when you need it doing. That costs money and doesn't happen by accident.

For example, it may be strategically important to have a more experienced manager when the business reaches a certain number of personnel. In that scenario, the strategies you can employ will be either short term (recruitment) or longer term (if you have time, complete training and development). It is up to you to decide the best course of action as the business leader.

Strategically important action in terms of people will always be focused on boosting capacity and competence; in other words, the capability to deliver your Future State. Your business can be viewed as an intricate machine, where each individual is a component with a specific job to do, which, when combined with the other components, works like clockwork to bring about your Future State.

Unfortunately, your people are not machines (although some organisations that we've seen seem to treat their people that way). You can't just programme them with a task and expect them to get on with it. They need to understand how and why they contribute to the success of the business.

This is your "performance review" or "appraisal" process. We don't like those words, partly because they have become discredited in the eyes of business leaders, but mainly because they don't convey how strategically important this process is.

Inevitably, when we mention introducing such a process, we are rewarded with much rolling of eyes and groaning. Business leaders and employees alike treat it as some sort of 'bolt-on' that they really ought to do because their HR consultant or business adviser told them to. But without such a process (we will, reluctantly, call it a performance review process), you will find it *much* more difficult to reach your Future State and it will certainly take longer. Why is that?

Because, without it, your people will not know how they contribute to the success of the business. They won't know, specifically, what they need to do and when it needs to be done by. They won't know how you are going to support them, through training and development, to reach these objectives, or how you are going to reward them when they do.

If they fall behind, they won't know what process you have in place to help them catch up, or what happens if, consistently, they don't perform as expected. You won't know any of those things either.

Booster 1: Transparent Leaders

We spend most of our professional lives encountering business owners and entrepreneurs who feel that their employees aren't pulling their weight and are the cause of problems. When it comes to people performance we have always adopted the philosophy that if this is the case, it is always your fault.

There is no doubt that the people who work for you and with you can be extremely frustrating (they're only human after all). However, it is ultimately your responsibility to ensure those working for you possess the capability needed to reach your Future State.

As a business leader it is your responsibility to make sure your people:

- Clearly understand how they individually contribute to the success of the business.
- Have access to the best tools to perform their current role.
- Receive adequate management that explains exactly what you expect them to do.
- Are motivated and engaged.
- Attain the skills needed to perform their future role in the business – in line with the demands of your Future State.
- Are rewarded appropriately for achieving what you asked of them.
- Actually work for you and not a competitor!

It is sheer fantasy to expect an employee to be as committed as you in the business. It's not their Future State after all, it's yours! To waste energy being disappointed in people affects your entrepreneurial mindset and drags you into tactical thinking.

When you're up to your elbows in the day-to-day running of the business, it's easy to forget that you are the leader. That doesn't mean that you necessarily have to crackle with charisma, but you do need to lead.

To lead, you have to be going somewhere and purposefully take your people with you to your destination. It's not enough to expect them to follow you blindly. You have to tell them, clearly, concisely and continuously, where you are all going and how you are intending to lead them there.

You want them to follow you willingly, too, and not just for pieces of silver. You must lead by example (that doesn't mean emptying the waste paper bin), treat people as you expect to be treated and, most importantly, share your Future State in an appropriately edited way.

Most businesses that have adopted the Game Change approach produce an employee-friendly version of their Future State, which is then displayed on the walls of their offices and presented to their staff.

We don't ask them to do this. That is what they think works best.

Once again it's up to you to interpret what is the best fit for your unique business environment.

Typically, an employee-friendly version only requires the removal of the personal elements within the Future Statement, for example playing more with the grand children or selling the business (probably likely to cause alarm!)

What remains is exactly what people need to know i.e., what success looks like and how their actions contribute to the bigger picture.

The Future State gives people added meaning in their daily tasks, just as it gives you added meaning in yours.

Your people realise that even though they may be a very small cog in a very big wheel, every single turn is important to your mutual success.

On a personal level the people in a business have three base concerns:

- How much am I paid?
- When will I be paid?
- How long will you keep paying me?

An employee does not have the freedom to rapidly inflate their income so their remuneration must cover all the costs to support their family, their lifestyle, and move them towards their own individual future state e.g., owning a house, paying for holidays. That means any signs of uncertainty in the leadership can be incredibly debilitating to their work as worry saps their energy.

The knock-on effect is that the employee then searches elsewhere for added security from alternative employers.

In that scenario you *unexpectedly* lose capability. When people leave your organisation at a time of their choosing and not yours, the result is unplanned disruption, delay and unforeseen costs.

All three of these factors will delay the arrival at your Future State.

In this respect you must prove to people that you have a credible plan for the future which, by default, supports their own future.

The hardest workers can be found in businesses with the best leaders, as the employees can plainly see there is a greater design, a plan, and that we aren't just making it up as we go along. Your Future State document is that proof. Don't keep it a secret.

Booster 2: Marvellous Management

HERMAN®
© LaughingStock Licensing Inc.

"I think my test results are a pretty good indication of your abilities as a teacher."

Just as people want to know how they fit into the bigger picture, they are also equally concerned with their place in the *here and now*.

We have already stated that any failures in people performance are your responsibility and, if applicable, the managers you appointed. In every business there is no excuse for poor management.

That means you must implement a review process, as we mentioned earlier, to ensure everyone always understands what their roles and responsibilities are. It also means constant and appropriate training, academic and practical (shadowing).

Importantly, reviews should not be a blame game as the real purpose is to maintain a constant dialogue with the people who are performing vital tasks. As such, it must be a two-way process and is as much a tool for your people as a business tool for you.

Your people must feel able to speak up if they need more help or can see an opportunity for improvement, not in a random way, but at regular planned intervals.

That shouldn't stop you chatting to them informally as you pass the working day. In fact, that is an important part of the whole process.

In our experience, most managers unintentionally create a negative culture because they do not appreciate that the buck stops with them. The chain of command is there for a reason, so that a named individual can assume responsibility for the actions and capability of others.

It is your responsibility to recognise any deficiencies in that management and address these using training and development strategies. Then, if your managers still fail after every chance has been given, they should find themselves managed out of the organisation, without question.

That is the level of threat that 'average' management is to your business. Poor performance in managers needs to be remedied rapidly because it only takes one poor manager to destroy your entire Future State.

If you're a sole trader, the same rules apply to you! If you can't manage people effectively, then find someone who can.

Booster 3: Mind the Gap

The purpose of training and development is to equip your people with the capability they need to achieve their objectives and to prepare them for the challenges they will face along the way.

Serendipitously, supporting people in this way – giving them the tools they need to succeed – makes them happy. A nice bonus!

"Start? Start what? I thought you said you hired me to take care of the books."

You must appraise a person's competence at regular intervals, benchmarking current ability against the level of skill needed to perform their role in the Future State. It becomes a race to be ready that requires investment in courses and qualifications of *your* choice. The Future State isn't a democratic movement. There is no gain if your people decide to become expert florists but your business is in engineering. You decide the development needs based on the needs of the business, not the individual. Skills gap analysis is another industry in consultancy that looks complex, but once again, how hard can it be?

As your review process becomes embedded, you will be able to establish a person's current competence, compare it against the skills you know they'll need in a year's time and invest accordingly in timely training, in line with your Future State.

Reviewing all your people in this way gives you a global oversight of the gaps, and the competencies required to achieve your Future State. If you are a sole trader, then you must apply the same principles vigorously to identify your own skills gaps.

We have lost count the number of times we meet entrepreneurs reluctant to train their staff in case they leave.

If your people do leave unexpectedly it isn't because you trained them. It is probably because you over-trained them without any thought about how that training was going to enhance their capability to accelerate you to your Future State. They do the training, become more motivated and then go back to exactly the same job that they did before.

The result is that they become demoralised and feel undervalued, both financially and mentally. It is unreasonable to expect people to show you unwavering loyalty just because you paid for some training. You have a responsibility to give your people real purpose and an opportunity to enjoy using their new skills.

Otherwise, quite reasonably, they will go elsewhere to satisfy their personal need. Be careful though. Skills gaps only need to be filled, not exceeded.

Alternatively, if you take the other view and invest in training beyond the level needed to fill the skills gap, do so in the expectation that you will generate a much higher return on investment for a shorter period, at which point that person will exit and you will need to recruit a replacement.

In our experience the most successful entrepreneurs adopt this policy, continuously exceeding the skills gap, enjoying bursts of excellence for shorter periods rather than competence for a longer term.

These business leaders see departure to another employer as the natural end to the training and development process.

Of course, when adopting this strategy, it is vital you are always developing a replacement. People are expected to leave, even encouraged to do so, but by design and not by accident, at a time of your choosing.

Regardless of the strategy you select, meeting skills gaps or exceeding them, accept that people owe you no loyalty in business.

That belief will spare you a lot of angst as an entrepreneur.

Employees are paid a wage to produce an output. You're not doing them a favour. Employment is a mutual and equal transaction.

Warning: Family and Friends

The chances of realising your Future State are intrinsically linked to making the right decisions when it comes to key workers and capability. Therefore, employing your friends and family represents a significant threat to your business.

To achieve your Future State, it is critical you have the right people, with the right skills at the right time. You also have to make sure your people are in roles that allow them to use their competence.

You rarely have this luxury in family businesses where roles are inherited and over promotion is common.

No one wants to cause family friction or breakdown, so the following statement should be taken with that caveat. However, in business there is no excuse for retaining people who cannot deliver what is required.

To do so compromises your Future State and undermines everything you are trying to do.

When P.T. Barnum describes people as "living resources" he does so unemotionally because that is what great decision-making in business demands.

We are certainly not suggesting you should start sacking your loved ones or making your mother redundant. However, we are highlighting that if you decide to make an emotional compromise and retain family and friends in key roles, you must recognise the resulting impact on your Future State. You must then take additional action to compensate for any shortfall in performance.

If family or friends are in management and create a negative impact on culture (or brand), there can be no compromise and they must be managed out of those roles.

'Promotion' into a less damaging job is a way to achieve the desired effect, while avoiding potatoes being thrown at you over Sunday lunch.

Booster 4: Tools of the Trade

It doesn't matter how much you increase the knowledge and competence of your people if you give them poor quality tools to perform the tasks.

"Haven't you got a brush?"

If your performance is heavily dependent on computers, make sure you know when the equipment is becoming outdated and invest in the best. If you don't, the competition will.

If your performance is heavily dependent on transport, make sure you have the best vehicles that drive with maximum fuel efficiency.

Supplying people with the best tools of the trade keeps them happy and raises the chance of getting a return on your investment in training and development.

Poor workers may blame their tools, but poor business leaders blame their workers. It's just too easy to assume people are the problem.

Ultimately, you determine the quality of the tools. It's hard to be a great artist using a toothbrush. It's not impossible, but most will struggle.

Who's the one shirking responsibility in that scenario? It's you. First check whether the tools you supply your workers are the best they can be. Then question competence.

Money is not Motivation

We can count the number of people that we have met who were truly motivated simply by money on the fingers of one hand. However, we have met many who were most definitely demotivated by money, for example, poorly implemented bonus systems.

It is vital your reward strategy is a fair reflection of the competence, time and commitment invested by personnel. Fairness is all you need to achieve in this respect; it is not necessary to throw more money at a person than is needed to keep their morale intact and committed to working for you.

"You can earn £504 a week if you work the full 168 hours."

A classic example of the misguided belief that only money motivates is when managers are promoted to Directors. Typically, their reward package includes some sort of share ownership in the hope that this creates extra commitment.

Let's be clear about the value of equity in any business. It should never be used as a form of payroll, unless facing truly exceptional circumstances. The only scenario we can envisage where this action might be appropriate is when a business is experiencing a severe cash flow shortfall and is in imminent danger i.e., you can't afford to meet payroll in cash. Of course, if you implement the Future State effectively you will never have to face that nightmare scenario.

There are two excellent reasons why you should think very carefully before using equity as payroll. Firstly, you only have a finite number of shares and when you transfer them to another person that is a one-time only deal. You can't do it again. Secondly, the more of your company you give away, the less you have for yourself, which means a smaller pay-out if your Future State is dependent on an exit through a sale.

It's better to implement a reward system based on performance which will, if devised and implemented wisely, always be an incentive. That way the individual receives a share of the spoils for their actions, rather than a share of your Future State! Any person who has faith in their own capability will accept this type of offer.

A word on bonuses. In our experience, this is often the reward system favoured most by business and it is certainly very prevalent. However, nearly always the bonus becomes an expectation, which means if you decide not to pay it for whatever reason, you will find you have a host of disgruntled and demotivated people. Think very carefully before introducing a bonus system and ask yourself whether you are doing it for the right reasons and not because it is relatively easy to introduce.

When it comes to reward strategies we are particularly fond of P.T. Barnum's take on the topic, written way back in 1880:

"If, as they get more valuable, they demand an exorbitant increase of salary; on the supposition that you can't do without them, let them go.

Whenever I have such an employee, I always discharge them; first, to convince them that their place may be supplied, and second, because they are good for nothing if they think they are invaluable and cannot be spared. But I would keep them, if possible, in order to profit from the result of their experience. For those people who have brains and experience are not to be readily parted with; it is better for them, as well as yourself, to keep them, at reasonable advances in their salaries from time to time."

The Recruitment Dilemma

HERMAN®
© LaughingStock Licensing Inc.

**"This is the new man, Hawkins. Teach him
everything you know, then pick up
your severance cheque."**

Once you identify a current or future skills gap between what you need to do and the capability of the people you already have, you will have the choice of three strategically important actions:

1. If time permits, train and develop existing personnel and backfill their roles as needed.

2. If tight time scales and complexity make training the high risk option, look outside the business and recruit ready-made people who already have the capability you need.

3. Change your Future State - if you do not create the capability needed in your people, including you, it is impossible to reach your destination!

As people strategies go, recruitment is the most risky, disruptive, and expensive if you get it wrong. That applies whether you outsource your recruitment or choose to use an internal process.

We can appreciate how following a structured recruitment process, under the control of an outside agency, may seem a better route to find the right person for a role. However, in our experience, businesses frequently have to go through two or even three rounds of costly (in time and money) interviews using this 'arranged marriage' approach. This outcome is hardly surprising when you have effectively delegated responsibility for assembling the beauty parade to someone with minimal sector experience who doesn't know your company intimately, applying science, not instinct, to select the right person.

Whilst this may be an uncomfortable truth for many, the most effective recruitment strategy we have witnessed in the field is the old fashioned head-hunt, or poaching. There's no nice word for it because it is inherently aggressive. In plain language you investigate your competitors' people and seek a match. You then incentivise that person to join your tribe instead. This strategy costs a premium in terms of salary.

You must also be able to communicate your Future State as switching employer is rarely a decision about short-term money and is frequently about a better existence and more potential in work. The premium paid is almost always less than the costs of an external agency and invariably generates a better match i.e., return on investment.

To explain, persuading a competitor's prize employee to join your team is more likely to work first time, as that person is culturally similar and working under the same pressures in a similar trading environment. In addition, head-hunted people bring with them capability that someone else has paid for (which means you offset any premium paid against training savings). Their track record is proven. Throw in the not insignificant bonus that they almost always bring new relationships with them (new customers and suppliers) and your Future State is suddenly looking much sunnier

The downside is, of course, that you're going to upset your competitors! We meet many entrepreneurs that maintain they don't have competitors because they all collaborate and get along. We always dismiss that as fanciful thinking as there is only a finite amount of new business available (see Chapter 3: Business Life and Death). Be in no doubt that, when push comes to shove, your competitors will try to take your customers. It's not a malicious trait as your fellow entrepreneurs have their own families to support and must rightly put them first. To use the old cliché, it's not personal, it's just business.

Warning: before implementing a head-hunting strategy you should pause and consider very carefully what your competitor's reaction may be. If the level of response jeopardises the Future State, then don't do it. A number of years ago we worked with an entrepreneur who determined to literally destroy a smaller competitor for the simple reason that they were irritated by them. We pointed out that there was no Future State gain by investing in such a micro strategy, but by then it was no longer about finance, it was about emotion, punishment and in their eyes, justice. Therefore, it's always a good policy in business to avoid making enemies if you can, especially ones with more resources at their disposal!

However, *if* your Future State depends on it, you should make this decision unemotionally and without hesitation. After all, it is not your responsibility to keep other competitors' staff happy. If an employee wants to leave, that is their right.

Finally, be very aware that this whole strategy can just as easily work in reverse! In that scenario your only defence to a raid on your people is to ensure that they love working for you. Money will be no defence at all.

KEEP IT SIMPLE TO SUCCEED

1. Review your Future State and Strategically Important Actions in Marketing and Sales, and Process.

2. What are the key worker roles needed to achieve your future state?

3. What skills and experience do these people need (capability)?

4. Are these people already working in the business?

5. If not, what are you going to do about it and when?

6. Devise a people review process that fits with the culture of your business and implement it.

Your ideas must be ABOVE and BEYOND what you already do in terms of people improvement and must contribute to your Future State.

Chapter 10
Above and Beyond: Money

**"I don't want to worry you, but the guy
who delivered the pizza is your
financial planner."**

Every enterprise needs money to fuel their journey. The more money you have, the more things you can do.

The faster you travel, the sooner you will arrive at your Future State. This statement applies equally whatever your line of business, including charities and other not-for-profit organisations.

Yet, in our experience, the vast majority of entrepreneurs do not possess either the skills or inclination to prepare and interpret financial information and to use this information to make better decisions. As a result, we believe that the current approach to finance training is not fit for purpose, at least not for entrepreneurs.

On one hand the plethora of Finance for the Non-Financial courses are too factual and mechanical. On the other, those entrepreneurs who can afford their own professional accountants are bombarded with figures and analyses, making the data overwhelming and too complicated to interpret.

Based on first-hand experience, we would estimate that less than 5 per cent of the entrepreneurs we have worked with could truly read a Profit and Loss account and understand how to turn it into a living tool to make great decisions. That's not good enough.

Yet the concept of profit and loss is not a new one. For centuries it has been the foundation of measuring the financial performance in business.

The reason we need a grasp of the financials is not to report to the Government or please the bank manager (although you do have to do that!). The primary purpose is to help us make more money for doing the same thing.

When we make more good decisions than bad, we generate surplus profit and accelerate the journey to the Future State.

That is why finance must always be a strategically important action.

Caution: Business and life are not straight lines.

You realise by now that any forecast is out of date as soon as we commit it to paper, because the act of business is not static, it is constantly shifting in response to thousands of variables. However, while accepting this fact, you can still use assumptions to create scenarios that improve your decision making.

INCREASE THE MARGIN
STRATEGY 1: Influence the Cost of Existence

Even if you sold nothing for 12 months, at the end of the year you will have spent money.

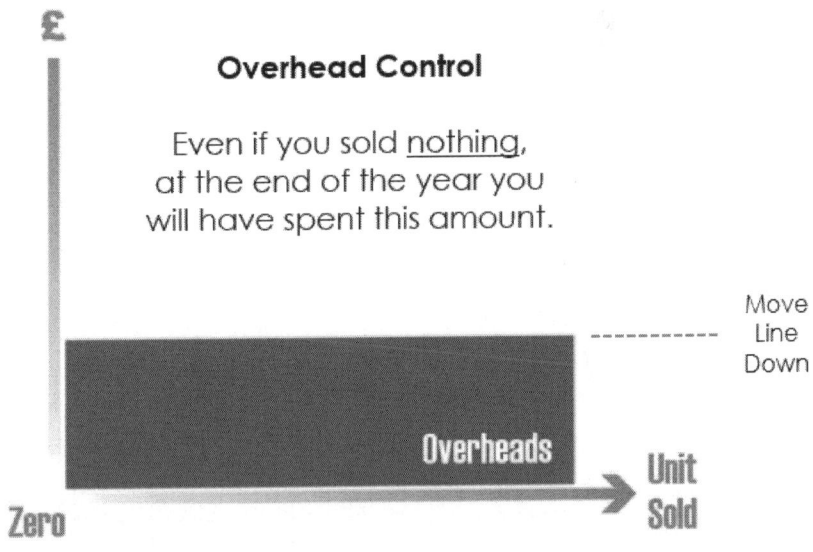

If you have no sales, you have no need to produce (or deliver) any products or services. Therefore, the only costs incurred would be those that enable us to be in business in the first place – office costs, people on payroll, utilities, professional fees and other administration.

You know these *costs of existence* (or overheads) because the expenditure is already taking place, otherwise you would be incapable of performing the act of business.

You should always be considering strategies to reduce the overheads as they increase your risk of business failure. You do this by renegotiating or substituting old for new. You may move to a lower priced accountant. You might relocate to new offices with lower rates and rent. Or you may choose to outsource and make people redundant.

None of these choices are easy decisions or strategies to implement. However, every time you reduce the costs of existence you reduce your exposure to risk and add money directly to the bottom line i.e., increasing profit or reducing losses depending on your current position.

There is one extremely important caveat to this strategy - never reduce the costs of existence if it means compromising the value added for a customer or jeopardising your brand promise.

The goal is to make more money for doing the same thing, by reducing costs and maximizing value to a customer, not to make the business inflexible and uncompetitive in the market place.

In those circumstances, your action might save money in the short term but effectively it is the catalyst for a long, drawn out commercial suicide.

INCREASE THE MARGIN
STRATEGY 2: Influence the Cost of Doing

Ignore the costs of existence for a moment. When you sell a product or service it immediately starts creating a new type of cost in the business – the cost of doing.

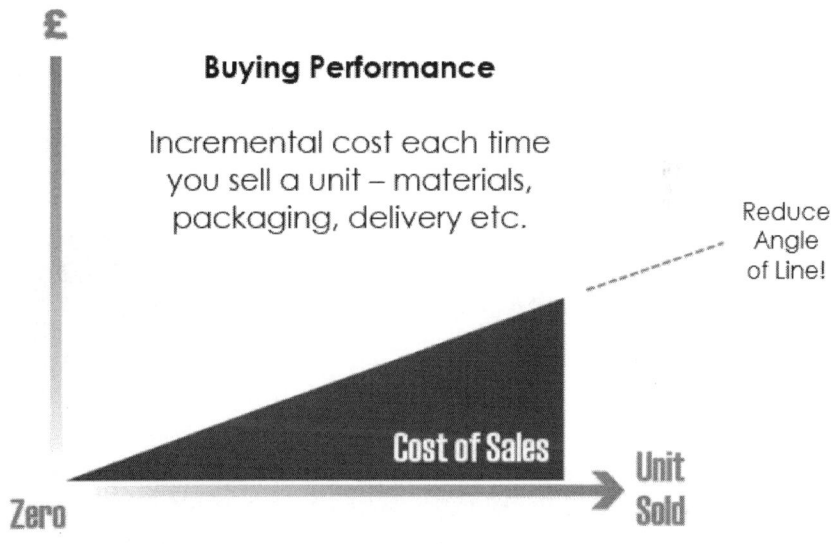

Once you have received an order, the product or service has to be delivered. That may mean purchasing materials or subcontract labour. It may mean physically delivering the item to the customer (petrol/courier). Transaction fees may be taken by your bank on receiving payment.

All of these costs would not have been incurred if you had not made the sale.

If you produce an identical product, the costs go up incrementally by the same amount each time you make a sale i.e., to produce and deliver another unit. This principle applies to all businesses, albeit they are likely to have a range of differing products and services in play.

Reducing the cost of doing, the amount of money spent to fulfil customer orders, instantly increases profit margin as we are effectively producing the same thing for less money. Strategies that influence the cost of doing include renegotiating supplier rates and the price of labour (if using sub-contractors).

This objective is much simpler to achieve than you might think. Your suppliers have fought hard to win your business and they know that the costs of attracting a new customer far outweigh the costs of keeping an existing one. At regular intervals you should contact suppliers and ask if they can offer better deals, because their competitors are doing everything they can to win your business. Far from penalising and bullying your suppliers, you're actually doing them a favour as they would much rather have a chance to keep you as a customer than just wake up one day to find you've moved on.

Another strategy to reduce the cost of sale is to improve productivity, i.e., generate more using the same amount of inputs (resources). That may require investing in better tools of the trade, new software or training. While not strictly a financial strategy (see Chapter 8: Above and Beyond Process) these strategies do lower the relative cost of doing, as labour cost per unit falls.

When you manage to reduce the cost of doing, the resulting margin gain is accrued each and every time you make a new sale. This is bonus profit that is added directly to the bottom line – more money for doing the same amount of work.

Putting it all together

Total costs = the costs of existence (overheads) + the cost of doing (sales)
... *at a given point in time*

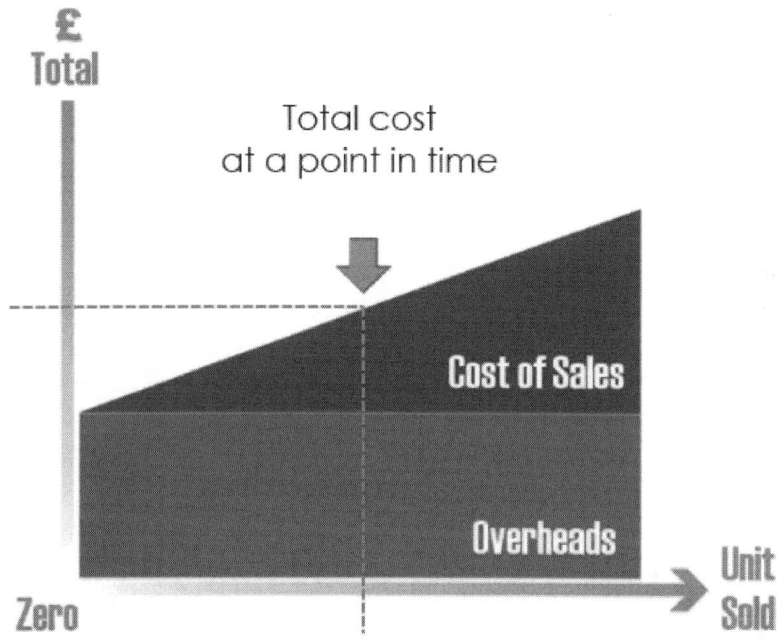

When it comes to the Future State you must have an instinctive grasp of the financial impact of your decisions. If you decide to increase sales, how much more cash must you find to fund this added amount of doing? If you are considering relocating to new premises, what impact will any cost savings have on your net profit? There isn't a *single* decision you make as an entrepreneur that shouldn't be linked to improving the financial performance of the business.

You don't need to be an accountant to work out the costs of existence and doing, just check your bank statement and bills. However, you do need to have access to reliable numbers and make sure you don't overload yourself with financial noise i.e., data that is superfluous to your needs.

Other than the gross profit rate, we seldom use ratio analysis, the preferred method of accountants, when helping entrepreneurs to understand their financial position. In reality, that level of detail soon becomes fiction, as the act of business includes so many different variables, tangible and intangible, that occur every day in an organisation. Less is more when you need to support your decision making as an entrepreneur.

The intention behind financial analysis is to highlight areas in your accounts to think about, but you don't need to over-complicate.

When I first became a business adviser, I struggled with the enormity of financial analysis and approached a colleague for help. He was formally PA to the Chief Executive of Barclays Bank and his answer was an epiphany to me – "just look down the profit and loss sheet, pick out the three biggest numbers and do something about them". Now *that* is a 'Finance for the Non-Financial' course in one sentence.

What could be simpler, more powerful and within the capability of all entrepreneurs? Nothing.

INCREASE THE MARGIN
STRATEGY 3: Influence the Price

We are fairly sure you have got the message by now; raising the perception of added-value in your brand means customers willingly pay more for the same product or service.

That difference between what you charge now and the potential price, goes straight on the bottom line. You make increased net profit every time you sell a product or service. That is the strength of brand power.

In our experience, most entrepreneurs fail to appreciate their real worth in the eyes of customers. As a result, they typically adopt pricing policies based on what their competitors are charging, not what a customer is willing to pay. Adopting a competitor-led pricing policy means every time you make a sale you are effectively throwing money away because of the missed income you could have earned if you had priced optimally.

Raising prices is definitely not a decision that should be taken lightly. If possible, you should ask your customers what they value most and test the market, for example, raising prices for a small, pilot group of customers off radar. Regular market research helps you monitor the current worth of products and services to a customer.

You adjust prices accordingly.

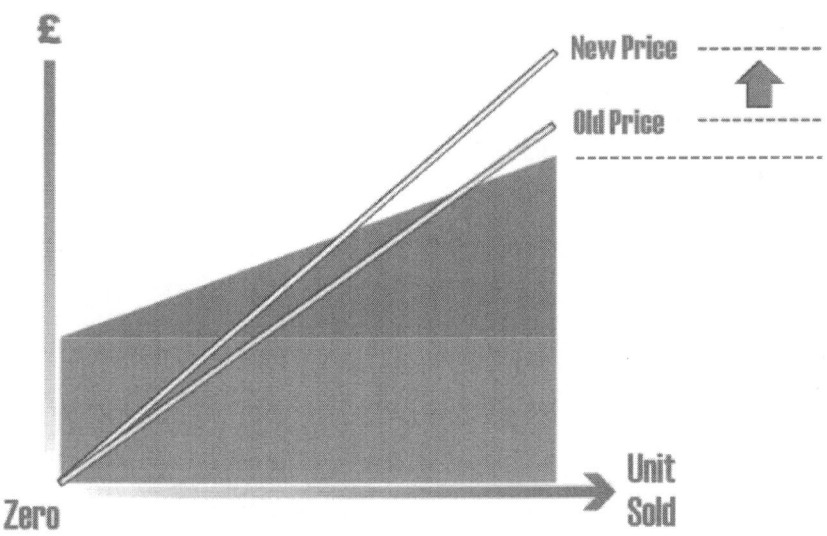

We also meet many entrepreneurs who insist they don't feel comfortable raising prices, as the amount their products cost to make means it wouldn't be fair to customers.

Let's get this straight right now. Using a cost plus 'a bit of profit' approach to pricing is incredibly limiting to business growth, reducing the chances of realising your Future State.

It's not up to you to decide what a customer feels and thinks, that's up to them. If a customer values what you do sufficiently to complete the transaction and be happy, then that is the value, not what you think it is.

You need to know what your customers think and let them decide the value, because if you can increase the price of an item without raising cost, it adds profit to the bottom line for doing exactly the same thing. That's a no brainer in any business.

The Broken Even Trap

The illustration on the previous page is the 'break even chart'.

It has historically always been presented as a way to know your break even point, in other words, how many units you need to sell to cover the costs of existence and doing.

While it does indeed provide that information, we're not very comfortable with the entire philosophy of break even, as it is a negative driver. As a result that is not the primary value in this chart at all.

As you have seen, it is entirely within your own capability as an entrepreneur to construct your own chart by adding up your costs.

Your role is to implement strategies that create as much profit as possible, not to break even. Knowing your survival target won't help you sleep at night! You need to aim higher than that to reach your Future State.

A Special Mention

Whilst not strictly a strategy to improve business performance, the cost of borrowing cannot be ignored as it can easily be the death of a business.

Our view is that you should constantly be looking for opportunities to renegotiate better deals on any debt to reduce the interest burden and cash payments. That money is straight out of the business and squeezing your cash flow, your working capital, the life blood of every business.

When it comes to lending and borrowing finance, once again we defer to the age-old opinions of P.T. Barnum:

"There is scarcely anything that drags a person down like debt.

Debt robs a person of their self-respect, and makes them almost despise themselves. Money is in some respects like fire; it is a very excellent servant but a terrible master.

When you have it mastering you; when interest is constantly piling up against you, it will keep you down in the worst kind of slavery.

Do not let it work against you; if you do there is no chance for success in life so far as money is concerned.

John Randolph, the eccentric Virginian, once exclaimed in Congress:

'Mr. Speaker, I have discovered the philosopher's stone: pay as you go.'

This is, indeed, nearer to the philosopher's stone than any alchemist has ever yet arrived."

Avoid Debt. The Golden Rules of Money Making. P.T. Barnum (1880).

KEEP IT SIMPLE TO SUCCEED

1. Review your Future State and Strategically Important Action in Marketing and Sales, Process, and People needs.

2. What opportunities are there for raising prices?

3. What opportunities are there for achieving savings in the costs of doing and reducing costs of existence, without compromising value and brand?

4. What do you need to do?

5. When?

Your ideas must be ABOVE and BEYOND what you already do in terms of financial improvement and must directly contribute to realising your Future State.

Chapter 11
Filling In Your Future State

**"I like a man who knows
where he's going."**

It is now time to complete your Future State. Do not overcomplicate or overthink it, just write a brief statement in each box. A blank template can be viewed on page 229 of this book. The Future State template can also be downloaded online at www.gamechangebook.com.

Your Future Statement should be surrounded by the four Strategically Important Actions you need to do brilliantly, every time, to make it a business reality.

Remember, you don't have to have one of each type, i.e., brand/sales and marketing, process, people and money. If your aspiration demands four brand building strategies, then that's right for your business.

It is important to understand that your decisions do not have to be 100% correct at this stage, as your template will evolve as you go on to test any assumptions in the coming weeks. You will make adjustments as necessary. However, it is critical you put something down on paper now that captures your current thinking.

This first draft is the beginning of creating a Future State document that stands the test of time and is fit for purpose, not just today, but through to the end – the arrival at your ideal life in business.

If you are unsure at any point when completing the Future State template, please refer to the examples in Appendix C. These Future States have been completed by real entrepreneurs who have been through the Business Think Game Change programme.

It's important to note that there is no 'one size fits all' in business and the strategically important actions in the examples we have included rightly vary in complexity, timescale and personal goals.

Your document will be unique to you. There is no right or wrong.

The three horizontal dotted lines in the corners of the blank Future State Template should list the day-to-day activities that prove you are implementing the strategy. It is very easy to fall into a comfort zone, especially when business is going well, that everything is progressing as planned. If you cannot see physical evidence of these activities happening in your business, the strategy is not being implemented. This means you need to fix that situation immediately or you are falling behind plan.

Writing your Future State and Strategically Important Action is the easy bit. The hard bit is making it happen. In the next section, Act 3, we will give you a methodology to take your Future Statement and turn it into a powerful tool for steering your organisation. One that constantly drives you on and pushes you to do better, in good times and bad.

Decide your FOUR SIA and enter text into BOXES

+ Brand Power

SIA 1

SIA 2

INJECT POWER
(above and beyond)

SIA 3

SIA 4

ACT 3: CLEAR DIRECTION

Chapter 12
Being Crazy Isn't Enough

In the first two Acts of Business, we encouraged you to remain in an optimal Enterprise State, to be expansive and create strategically important action to game change your business (using the Pareto Principle). However, even the most effective entrepreneurs will fail to realise their Future State if they don't adopt a pragmatic approach to the day-to-day challenges of managing and directing business improvement.

Making it happen is going to be one of the scariest rides of your life. Therefore, we must use a simple approach to stay on course, because if we remain on track the challenges are greatly reduced.

You must think and act like a 'Board of Directors' to execute clear business direction. It doesn't matter whether you are on your own, a partnership or a global corporation; whoever is at the top holds ultimate responsibility for making the Future State a reality.

Company direction is not a new concept and successful businesses have used the same approach for hundreds of years. One of the most common errors you can make is to believe these rules don't apply to you because you don't have a global brand or think you can do it all instinctively. That route will create strategic drift and you will lose control.

As you already know, or will know soon if you are about to start a business, the challenges you face are massive in both practical and emotional terms and their impact is a constant threat to the direction of your business.

To put this in perspective, we have witnessed many lives suffer due to business pressures, personal relationships breaking down and illness. In 2009, we even received a suicide note from a customer (they lived).

Therefore, let us be very clear about our view on business and life. Business is a means to a great life, not the other way round. It is not the end of your life if your Future State fails, it's the end of a business.

So what? Just do something else.

That is the very essence of entrepreneurship – you own your destiny.

If at First You Don't Succeed...

The original reasoning behind the creation of bankruptcy law was to ensure that there is an arrangement with your creditors; that their debts are paid in whole or in part. That objective is still the primary purpose.

However, in modern times, there has been a movement to reduce the punitive period, with the intention of giving people a second chance.

It would be naïve to think the Government is having a caring moment. This safety valve allows you to start *another* business as quickly as possible, because the entrepreneur crop is critical to the country's success and is always in short supply.

The economy can't afford to lose anybody with entrepreneurial skills, especially those with hard-earned battle experience.

Obviously it's a better idea to avoid this scenario in the first place!

In the words of the writer and philosopher, Dr. Seuss: "Being crazy isn't enough". That's why you need clear business direction.

"Being Crazy Isn't Enough..."

A Living Document

You have defined a Future State to create your ideal life in business. That serves as a constant reminder why you come to work every day and put yourself through the challenges. You have defined four strategically important actions (SIA) which, if constantly improved and done brilliantly every time, will inject exponential power into your journey.

You may be able to afford to take your eye off other aspects of the business, but you can never neglect these four critical Core Contributors. You have listed three 'activities' for each that are indicators the strategies are being implemented, for example, promotion for marketing and sales.

At the moment these are just words. Now you need to turn the Future State Template into a living document, one that isn't destined for the back of the drawer. The Future State should be a tool you use every single day to direct your organisation. Otherwise, inertia and strategic drift will kill your journey.

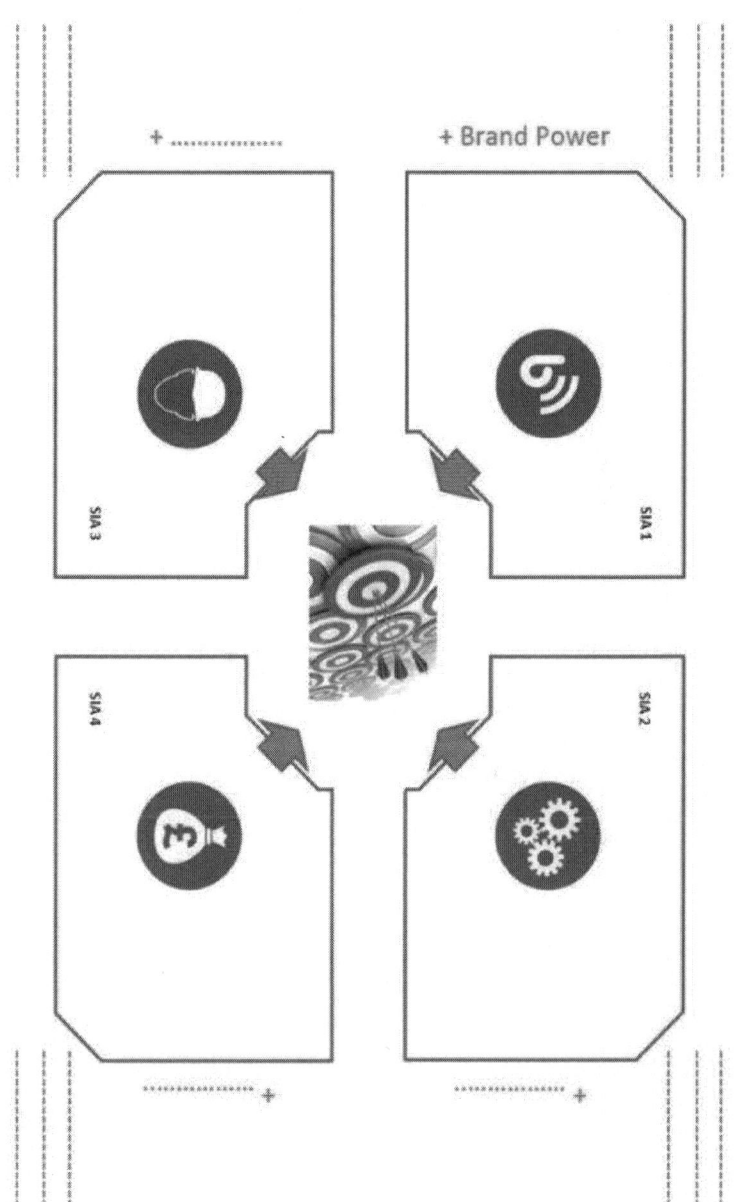

+ ....

+ Brand Power

SIA 3

SIA 1

SIA 4

SIA 2

+ ....

+ ....

What is Strategic Drift?

Strategic drift is being pulled off course as a business, not consciously but unconsciously. You don't realise you're off course until the damage is done. There is no larger threat to your Future State than strategic drift and you are the only person responsible for this happening. Worse still, this effect is most likely to happen when your business is performing well, not underperforming. So while you may be celebrating your achievement, your Future State is actually moving further away. How can this be?

We encourage all entrepreneurs to be opportunistic. After all that is the very essence of enterprise, to create opportunities. However, that doesn't give you an excuse to say yes to anything that makes money. That is being a maverick, not an entrepreneur. They're not the same.

A maverick - someone who refuses to adhere to the rules - is something we think every entrepreneur would like to be called at some point in their business life. However, once again, being crazy isn't enough. Successful enterprise is being creative enough to recognise the opportunities, but also pragmatic and bold enough to reject them - if they don't contribute to your Future State.

You need to be a leader, not a follower, to direct a business effectively. That may mean turning away money-making opportunities. That will feel contrary to every business bone in your body, but your Future State is designed to keep you honest and on the right path.

If an opportunity doesn't move you forward towards your ideal life in business (or out of it), then you have to ask yourself why you would invest precious finite resources and time in such a venture. That is an opportunity cost.

Generating a profit is not sufficient reason in itself to make a strategic decision as a business leader. Your actions must always contribute to the bigger picture and accelerate the Future State.

We have lost count of the number of wealthy entrepreneurs we have met in business who are miserable and unhappy. These people blindly followed the finance and put profit first, often ahead of their own family and work-life balance. In business terms these people appear extremely successful from the outside. Inside they have regrets. They are rich in cash terms, but failed to realise their Future State – an ideal life.

Don't make a similar mistake by thinking happiness and profit are synonymous. You need to think bigger than that and not blindly chase the money. If an opportunity doesn't contribute to reaching the Future State, reject it and look for another. Your time and resources can then be invested in the right places.

You only make informed decisions if you know exactly what you are aiming for (a Future State) and exactly where you are on the journey (direction). This process is at the heart of the Game Change approach and Future State philosophy.

Avoid strategic drift at all costs by using business direction. Keep your eyes open.

Your business depends on it.

The Importance of Hats

We have worked with many Boards of Directors who believe they share a group responsibility for the performance and progress of their organisation. This committee style approach is ineffective compared to assigning specific responsibility and accountability to an individual. Even great teams have leaders. Brilliant committees have Chairs. If everyone is responsible that means no one is.

That doesn't mean we are advocating a blame culture and finger pointing. Far from it, but if sales and marketing is a strategically important action to realise your Future State, there needs to be accountability. You must be able to challenge a named individual why progress hasn't been made. If you're on your own as a solo entrepreneur, you need to be brave and self-aware enough to challenge yourself!

The act of business has distinct functions that each demand a unique set of skills. There is a sequential order to the functions and, as a result, if there's a lack of progress in any single discipline, it affects the entire business. We all have the responsibility for making the Future State a reality, but the sheer scale of the act of business means we have to delegate certain responsibilities and trust others to deliver on their promises, the targets and progress required to reach our destination.

It is rare to find a business under £5 million turnover with the luxury of having a Director for each function, for financial reasons as much as anything else. That is a major challenge for the solo entrepreneur and small business. Most entrepreneurs simply won't have the money to fund the skills, experience and employment needed to assemble a full Board of Directors. Therefore, you will most likely be deficient in some of the critical functions needed to direct a business. That means you need tools to help you steer effectively.

We have worked with many sole traders who believe they can outsource or ignore some of the critical functions of directing their business. That approach is a serious threat to achieving your Future State, as a named individual must wear each of the business 'hats'.

If you are a solo entrepreneur and it's just you in the business, congratulations! You get to wear all the hats simultaneously! That's the harsh reality of your circumstances. However, the *order* you put the 'hats' on will be the difference between building a great business and not realising your potential.

Responsibility + Purpose = Action

With the functional Hats you generate added responsibility. The Future State gives you added purpose.

When you marry the two, results are exponential.

Chapter 13
The Purpose of Board Thinking

There is a significant amount of confusion when it comes to the act of business direction. In our experience, less than 5% of the entrepreneurs we have encountered employ these techniques.

Why would this be, when there are centuries of evidence proving that adopting a 'Board of Directors' approach increases your chance of business success?

Elitism and Insecurity

At the beginning of 2014 there were over 5 million businesses actively trading in the UK. 62% (3.3 million) were sole proprietorships, 29% cent (1.5 million) were companies and 9% (460,000) were partnerships.

Source: http://www.fsb.org.uk/stats Nov, 2014

The bastion of the Board of Directors has long been Companies House, who state you can only technically be a Company Director if your business is registered at that Institution. On that basis, only 1 in 3 are entitled to call their business a 'Company'.

We believe this definition fosters a belief system that, even though we are all entrepreneurs engaged in enterprise, the rules of direction do not apply to two-thirds of businesses. It implies that being a Director is somehow exclusive and reserved for a more sophisticated type of business – the registered company.

What the Institute of Directors Say

The purpose of a Board is:

"To ensure the company's prosperity by collectively directing the company's affairs, whilst meeting the appropriate interests of its shareholders."

Source: "Standards for the Board: Improving the Effectiveness of Your Board (Good Practice for Directors)" - Institute of Directors, 2002

Well *that* sounds exciting and engaging! Is it any wonder that entrepreneurs reject the need to think like a Board of Directors, when the 'champions' of the concept talk about business as if it was a machine? If you don't have other shareholders (you own the entire business), you haven't registered as a Company (71% of entrepreneurs don't) and aren't willing to talk like an accountant (no offence intended), why on earth would you think you belong to this club, or want to for that matter?

We have repeatedly stated that your purpose as a business leader is to create and reach a Future State that fulfils your *life* goals. We agree that you should be a servant to the business and view it as an entity in its own right. But the only difference between unregistered and registered (a Company) is that the latter is a separate legal entity, individual in its own right, validated in law.

What Sir John Harvey-Jones Says

The purpose of a Board is:

"It's all to do with creating momentum, movement, improvement and direction. If not taking the company purposefully into the future, who is? The answer is of course, no one."

Source: John Harvey-Jones. "Making it happen: Reflections on Leadership", 1988 (p 147)

The purpose of Board thinking isn't to sit around a table drinking coffee, it's to better drive the plan forward, to constantly create new opportunities and steer the business so that you don't veer off course. It's to own a Future State and make it happen.

We are confident that every entrepreneur would buy into that idea. Company, sole trader or partnership, it makes no difference whatsoever.

When you think and act like a Board, you have the tools needed to manage strategy and *turn your aspiration into reality* - as economically as possible.

You then arrive at your Future State by design, not by accident, avoiding strategic drift and boosting performance every day. Not just when you remember or there's a costly crisis. Board thinking enables you to systematically and proactively seek out new opportunities and counter threats, rather than reacting.

Therefore, Board thinking saves you money, boosts performance and increases your chances of success (a better life in business).

Far from being a complicated process demanding qualifications and decades of experience, the act of thinking like a Board is a simple step by step process founded on common sense. It's just not that common due to the culture of business in this country and the current Government approach to industrial policy.

Failing to think like a Board - to direct - is the most likely cause of not realising your potential, or worse, complete business breakdown. Whether you are a sole trader or multi-national company, you must think like a Board of Directors to effectively counter threats and create opportunities, not once a year, but in the inevitable onslaught of pressure that is business as usual.

In our experience, a lack of Board Thinking is the primary reason why over half of businesses fail within five years. *That* is the change needed.

Board thinking forces you to make time for the bigger picture. That is the added power, constantly seeking business improvement, not as an occasional event, but as a way of being.

Functional Responsibility

The 'hats' that need to be worn to perform the act of business effectively are Marketing and Sales, Operations, People and Finance.

We hope those words sound familiar as those are the areas of Strategically Important Action we asked you to select earlier. However, in addition there are two more functional roles needed to think like a Board of Directors.

If you are in manufacturing the act of procuring materials and labour may be so important that is demands its own 'hat'. You also need a leader, because someone has to orchestrate the proceedings.

Do not make the mistake of thinking you need six people, one for each function. As we stated previously, it is extremely rare for any business with less than £5 million turnover to have the payroll capacity to fund the employment of half a dozen Directors. The reality is that entrepreneurs in small and medium sized businesses have no choice but to wear multiple hats, with individuals being responsible and accountable for more than one area of the business.

If you are a sole trader, you have to wear *all* the hats – that's no easy task, as it is impossible for a single person to be an expert in everything. Therefore, you must be acutely aware of your weaknesses and compensate accordingly by buying in additional experience and expertise.

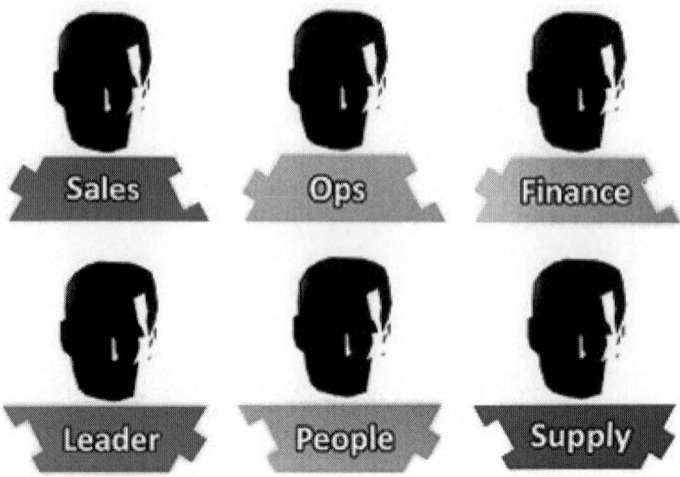

The functional responsibilities are not negotiable or optional, as they constitute the act of business itself.

Wearing *All* the Hats

If you are a sole trader or do not currently use other Directors in your business, you are effectively a 'One Mind Board'.

On the plus side you have a degree of control over all the functions. However, that benefit comes at a significant cost to the growth potential of your business.

Marketing and sales demands creativity, operations need process improvement, people asks for recruitment (and a legal awareness) and finance needs someone who can interpret data.

It is impossible to be expert in all the different skill sets needed to achieve excellence. For this reason, the ideal of a perfect entrepreneur does not exist. It's a myth.

When you have to wear all the hats your thinking becomes unbalanced, naturally focusing on those disciplines that are within your comfort zone, whilst other crucial functions in the act of business are not optimised. That decision is unlikely to be a conscious one.

When you wear all the hats you also have to deal with higher levels of stress as the entire thought process must be completed independently. You have to be aware enough to challenge your own thinking and in effect talk to yourself. That is the first sign of insanity in most circles, but in business, on your own, that's the way you stay sane.

You must know when to take off one 'hat' and put on the next. The *need for separation is vital* as thoughts become confused without order.

HAT 1: LEADER

Someone has to be in charge.

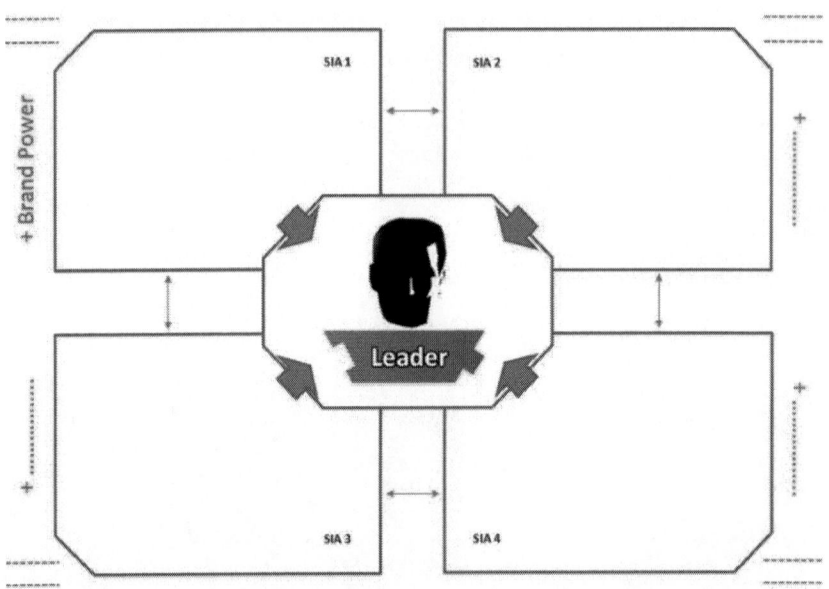

The equivalent role in the Boardroom is the Chair. This 'hat' orchestrates all of the other functions in the act of business.

This person is responsible for ensuring that 'stop and think' meetings on strategy take place at regular intervals and that sufficient information has been supplied in good time to make informed decisions at those sessions.

This role is also to be the 'face' of the business, representing the organisation and its brand externally. Without this critical function in the act of business there is no order, only chaos.

HAT 2: Marketing and SALES

The role of this 'hat' is to propose new opportunities to increase sales (and profit). It is also their responsibility to ensure the sales and marketing strategies currently being implemented are making progress at the expected rate and delivering the forecasted results.

HAT 3: OPERATIONS

This 'hat' must constantly be seeking out new opportunities to improve efficiency and productivity, to be able to do more with less. In parallel, this role must ensure the current systems and processes are fit for purpose and deliver the performance expected (to create the Future State).

HAT 4: SUPPLY

Not every entrepreneur will consider the function of supply to be a strategically important act of business. Another name for this 'hat' is Procurement. However, if the supply of materials (and/or labour) on time and at the best price is critical, a dedicated role is needed to constantly seek out the best sources.

HAT 5: PEOPLE

The People 'hat' is vital in every business. This role is responsible for personnel and must ensure the business has secured the right people, with the right skills, at the right time, in the right place. If you don't have employees, the goals are the same, but the people are outside your business.

HAT 6: FINANCE

Every business must always know where they stand with regards to money if they want to moderate risk and make effective decisions.

The Finance hat is responsible for presenting accurate information, for giving opinion on the current state of the finances and seeking out new opportunities to improve the financial strength of the business. As a result, any individual who dons the Finance hat is inherently unpopular, because it is their responsibility to be over-cautious and doubt every decision as if it might fail. In that respect, their role is the exact opposite of every other 'hat' in the Board Thinking process.

When you propose a great idea, this voice is the spoiler, the individual that slams on the brakes and says "no" when all around them are screaming "yes".

But there is no more important hat to wear than that of Finance. If your information is wrong, decisions are wrong. If your judgement and recommendation on whether the business can bear an investment is flawed, the decision is flawed. The Finance hat is the safety valve for your business that ensures your decisions are challenged fully and any resulting actions are based on fact, not fiction.

Whether you are on your own or in a twelve-person Board of Directors, how well you wear the Finance hat will make or break your Future State.

Are You Extra Special?

Some businesses require an extra special hat because their Future State depends on it. For example, if product development is a Strategically Important Action for your business, a named person must own the research and development function.

If you sell exclusively online then a hat should exist for e-business development, to ensure you never fall behind the fast moving technology. When Government contracts are vital to achieving your Future State then a named person must own the responsibility to nurture and exploit the relationships needed to deliver in this arena.

As before, 'one size fits all' does not apply in enterprise and, ultimately, the decision is yours on what is and isn't strategically important. However, to reach the Future State you must execute brilliantly. That means a logical order of thinking when it comes to the act of business and the need for discipline, particularly if you wear all the hats and have multiple roles.

Most importantly, every 'hat' must be worn by a named individual, someone that can say "the buck stops with me". That is how business leaders turn words (their Future State) into reality.

Individual accountability (HATS) = ADDED purpose + ADDED responsibility = MORE action.

KEEP IT SIMPLE TO SUCCEED

Which *named individual* 'OWNS' each hat in your business?
We can all contribute, but someone must have lead responsibility.

NB. You might wear them all!

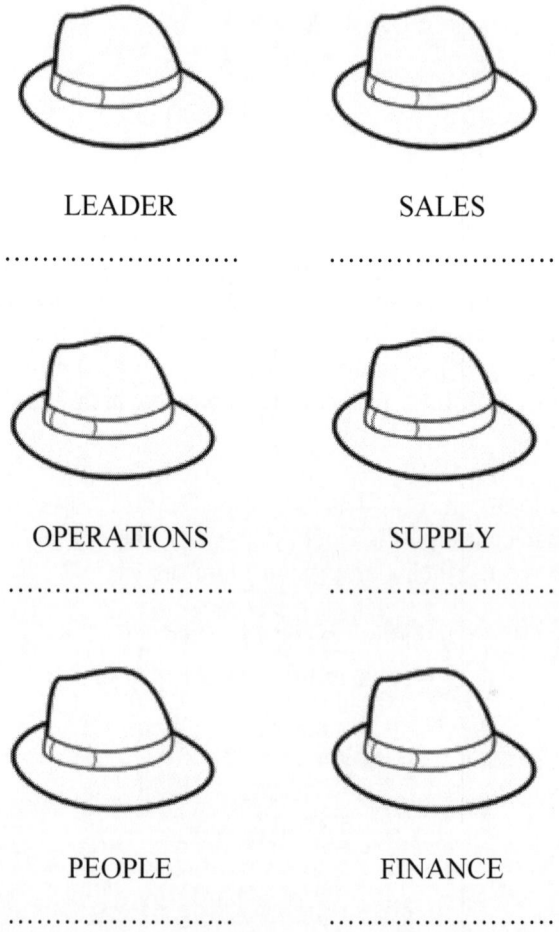

LEADER

....

SALES

....

OPERATIONS

....

SUPPLY

....

PEOPLE

....

FINANCE

....

Do you have, or do you need, a 'special' hat?

For example, technical, e-business, government, etc.

If any of your hats have been left blank, you need to address this situation urgently, as effectively no one in your business has responsibility for this function and is driving it forward. Worse still, no one is accountable for performance in the function.

If you wrote your own name under every hat, congratulations, you wear *all* the hats, you're the Board of One. Find some people to put on a few of your hats and lighten your load.

The sheer scale of the act of business means a named individual must have lead responsibility for the different functions.

Board thinking is the only methodology that has stood the test of time, bringing order to the intrinsically chaotic state that is business as usual.

The alternative, firefighting, is neither a strategy nor a happy place.

Chapter 14
Past Present Future

Successfully directing a business demands each functional hat performs a three step process.

1. The Past – did we make the expected progress?
2. The Present – can we deal with the immediate challenges?
3. The Future – can you identify opportunities/threats on the horizon?

It's as simple as that. If you answer no to any of these questions, then the business is behind plan. Your Future State is slipping. The purpose of the Game Change Approach is to embed a mindset and process that repeatedly challenges you to think past, present and future.

That is how strategic drift is prevented, by maintaining performance at the demanded levels and remaining acutely aware of impending threats and opportunities. Not reactively when there's a crisis, but proactively to avert the crisis in the first place.

Your Future Statement gives you the context and benchmark upon which to test the decisions. That is why you *must* make time for sessions on direction.

Challenge and Challenge Again

The difference between arriving at your Future State and finding yourself somewhere else is the quality of your decision-making along the way.

The act of business is dynamic, meaning we are constantly fighting a new set of unforeseen challenges at short notice. These events may be new competitors entering the market, key workers resigning, supplier bankruptcy or even our own health issues. The list is endless and you will continue to face these challenges throughout your business life.

How well you manage these events is the most important action you need to master in business, because at best they damage your Future State and at worst can destroy your business completely.

To put this in perspective, in 2010 we were supporting a glass maker who decided he wanted to introduce ceramics into the range. We challenged him why he would go down this route, when he had little experience of making ceramics and was better known in the market for glassware. We understood the end goal, to diversify and reach a new set of customers, reducing reliance on a single market. But the timing and capability readiness was wrong in our view. After a difficult discussion, the entrepreneur pressed on with his plan and invested heavily. Six months later, after many successful years trading in glass, a sizeable ceramic order went wrong in production and was cancelled. That single event killed the business in weeks, as it caused a cash flow crisis. As his livelihood unraveled, the entrepreneur said he could 'hear' my voice over and over in his head on the day the ceramics failed.

Every big decision you make needs to be subjected to scrutiny.

Ultimately, you control your own destiny and make the final decision.

Of course you won't always be right. However, the past, present and future test ensures you're right more times than you're wrong.

That's all you need to do to be successful.

SCENE 1: Review the Future Statement

Your Future Statement is not just words and window dressing.

If you have completed the 'Keep it Simple to Succeed' tasks in this book, you will have created a representation of what a happy life in business looks and feels like to you. You have produced an easy to understand plan outlining the four Strategically Important Actions that will inject exponential power into your journey.

The Future State is your road map to a better life and business.

Your resources will always be finite. There is only so much time available in the day and your people (contacts in and out of the business) are critical to every Future State. Therefore, when we pursue opportunities that don't contribute to reaching the Future State, we may make money but we veer off course. We can't get that time back, it's spent. This statement applies tenfold to your own use of time.

One of the critical responsibilities in 'Board Thinking' is to question every new opportunity and take nothing at face value. Before even evaluating the likelihood of success we must ask "does this course of action contribute to realising the Future State"? If not, why are we even considering the venture, if it doesn't move us closer, preferably faster, to the destination?

If you cannot answer that question adequately, reject it as an opportunity and say no. It didn't pass the 'if not, why' test.

This mindset is more important than you might at first think. As stated previously, being enterprising is inherently creative. It demands an ability to generate new ideas and seek out opportunities. However, there comes a time when we need to stop having new business ideas and knuckle down to turn the existing ones into business as usual.

Returning to P.T. Barnum, as entrepreneurs, we should all heed his warning:

"Be not too visionary. Every project looks to them like a certain success, and therefore they keep changing, always in hot water, always under the harrow."

Whether it's just you, or a room full of functional Directors, it is critical that any new ideas are challenged mercilessly to ensure they are fit for purpose, the purpose being to create our Future State as fast and economically as possible. The commitment to challenge is explicit, we expect it, invite it and embrace it. We all have a responsibility to speak up, because we know that failure to do so weakens our business.

We accept that there may be a set of exceptional circumstances where it is necessary to take on a profit-making opportunity outside the Future State, purely to help finance the business. However, that decision should never be taken lightly.

Chasing the money is the primary cause of strategic drift.

When it comes to entrepreneurship and enterprise, be constantly aware that your *time* is always more precious than *money*.

Before the start of any session on business direction, the Future Statement should be reviewed. That purpose reminds us *why* we are in the room.

SCENE 2: Execution – The Order of Hats

If you don't consider each function in the act of business sequentially this generates confusion.

In our experience, most entrepreneurs make the mistake of adopting finance as the dominant and lead function.

The reverse approach is true in high performing businesses.

<u>All the Hats in the Ring</u>

Let's revisit the functions needed to perform the act of business.

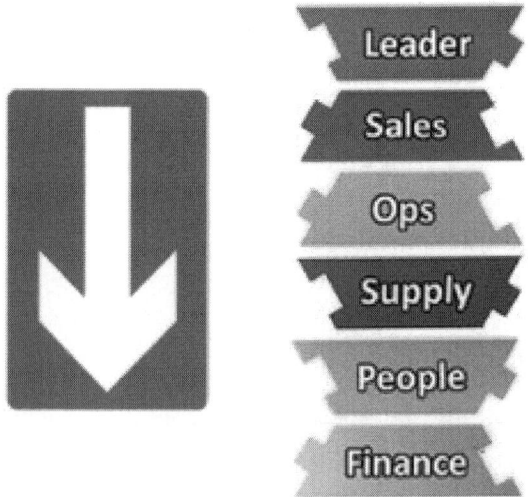

Board thinking should not be an unstructured debate. Without a set order, there is anarchy and conflict. It's not a brain-storming session. That was fine when we were creating the Future State. But now it's time to create business as usual.

As we have stated previously, a named individual must own each function (hat) for added accountability. In larger organisations these roles are called functional Directors. In small and medium sized businesses, you often have to wear multiple hats, or even all the hats if on your own, but *never* at the same time.

Failure to adopt a 'one hat at a time' approach causes confusion, lack of clarity, argument and poor decisions. A common sense order should be followed to ensure you get the best performance out of your organisation and reach the Future State.

1st: LEADER

The first act is scene setting. Someone has to be responsible for ensuring the meeting takes place in the first place, that the information needed is available and up to date, that there is an agenda and a conductor to orchestrate the discussion. In other words, a Chair. Running productive meetings always demands a strong chairperson and they are a rare commodity. This person must encourage people to speak out but shuts them down ruthlessly when they stray from the agenda. Their role in the order of hats is to present the Future State at the beginning of every session, as that is the benchmark for everyone.

2nd: Marketing and SALES (aka Business Development)

Next in order is the hat responsible for generating the demand needed to sell our products and services. It is vital that sales performance is maintained and new opportunities are constantly created.

The question at the heart of this role is *how can we sell more at a higher profit margin?*

3rd: OPERATIONS (OPS)

When the Sales function identifies new opportunities, the business needs to deliver that promise to the customer in terms of products and/or services. The level of challenge for the Operations hat is determined by the performance of marketing and sales. There is no point targeting a profit-margin and winning new orders if the business cannot physically deliver that performance, financially or practically.

The question at the heart of this role is *how can we do more for less?*

4th: SUPPLY

This hat may be sometimes be combined with Operations.

Once again, the challenge of procuring materials and labour is directly determined by the level of performance in the *sales* function. If we have more orders, we need more resources to deliver the products and services (material/labour).

The question at the heart of this role is *how can we ensure continuity of supply at the best price?*

5th: PEOPLE

The people we need, in terms of capability (competence + capacity), is directly determined by how we choose to do *operations*. The processes we create and complexity of performing those tasks dictates the skills needed and number of people that must be employed.

The question at the heart of this role is *how can we ensure we have the right people, with the right skills, at the right time, in the right place?*

6th: FINANCE

The amount of finance needed to fuel the act of business is directly influenced by performance in *marketing and sales*, *operations*, *supply* and *people*. Ensuring there is working capital available to spend and that the business is profitable is critical to both survival and realising your Future State.

However, starting with what you can afford is limiting, setting practical and psychological glass ceilings on what you can achieve as a business. Far better to decide what the business needs to do to reach your Future State and then determine a way to pay for it. That is enterprise. For this reason, the function of Finance is always *last* in the order of hats, but *first* in the order of importance.

The question at the heart of this role is *how to most profitably fund the act of business, now and in the future?*

In summary, one hat at a time…

1. LEADER   Present the Future State

2. SALES   How can we sell more at a higher profit margin?

3. OPS   How can we do more for less?

4. SUPPLY   How do we ensure continuity of supply at the best price?

5. PEOPLE   How can we ensure we have the right people, with the right skills, at the right time, in the right place?

6. FINANCE   How to most profitably fund the act of business, now and in the future?

That sequence should form the *permanent agenda* for *every* discussion you have on business direction.

The Perfect Meeting: PAST

We will be using the Sales hat to illustrate Board thinking in practice. However, the 'past present future' order applies to all the roles.

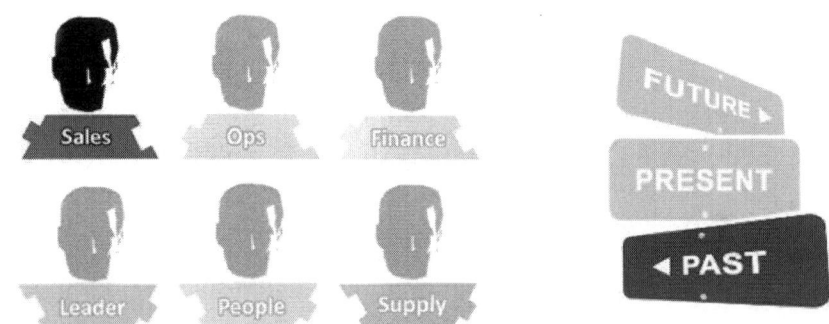

Each individual function must report progress against expected objectives. Otherwise, how can we know we are behind schedule? For example, if the Sales hat predicted an increase in unit sales of 10 per cent last month, we need to know that forecast has become a reality.

This information is absolutely critical when you consider the 'Order of Hats' knock-on effect. Failing to realise predicted sales performance will directly and immediately impact on the challenges faced by all the other hats in the act of business.

Underperformance in sales causes unused production capacity (waste), excess stock held (cash tied up), underused skills (needless training) and, most critically, a hole in the predicted financial performance of the organisation. That alone can be enough to destroy your business in less than 30 days, hence the need to have sessions on direction at least once a month.

In the process of thinking like a Board, the PAST comes first because what just happened is the most significant and immediate threat to business continuity.

The person who owns the Sales hat must have accurate data and be ready to present the results achieved since the last update, highlighting any gaps (positive or negative) between what was promised and what came to pass. That is the essence of gap analysis, recognising when a variation has occurred, understanding why and fixing it.

Be careful what you promise in terms of sales performance, as the other Hats in the ring are following your lead.

It is your sole responsibility to have the answers for the function you own, whatever hat (s) you may wear. Therefore, when challenged, you must be able to explain why performance has exceeded or failed to reach the target.

The Perfect Meeting: PRESENT

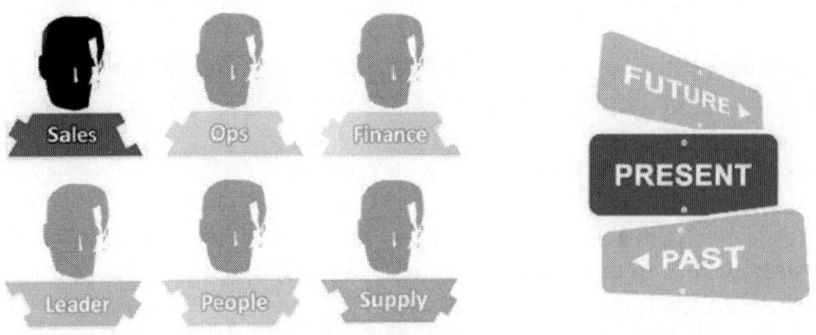

Once progress against forecast performance has been explained, you must then highlight any current challenges facing the organisation. Again, 30 days is typically the best period between direction sessions. That is an amount of time long enough for progress to be made (to have something to talk about) but sufficiently short enough to prevent any failures progressing unchecked (ensuring internal weaknesses do not transform into threats).

Examples of strategically important PRESENT updates from the Sales hat may be the closure of an external marketing agency, any customer changes due to an event in the news (brand damage) and the unexpected departure of key sales staff. There is no definitive list.

Any challenges faced in the sales function directly and immediately flow through the order of hats. You must ensure all the functions are informed.

When updating, each hat should be able to complete the Past and Present elements of their function in less than 10 minutes. If you cannot do this, then you are including too much management information. Reams of data can sometimes help maintain performance in business as usual (a management responsibility), but information overload has no place in discussions on the direction of the Future State.

To put this in perspective, when we work with Boards of Directors our opening move is always to observe a session. Afterwards, we ask for the written minutes of the discussion. Then we return a new version with all the day-to-day comments slashed through with red pen. Usually, about 75% of what is discussed has no place in a direction session. It is this rehearsal of day-to-day noise that complicates, clouds and compromises strategic thinking. Typically, removing these items reduces meeting times from three hours to one hour. That demands a strong Chair. Or if you are on your own, self-discipline.

If you can't do the entire hats process in ninety minutes, you're not focused. If you want to discuss day-to-day, do it somewhere else, such as a managers' meeting.

The Perfect Meeting: FUTURE

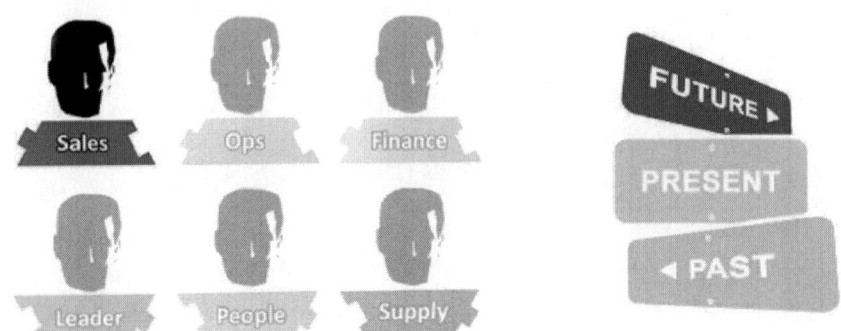

The Past and Present were the easy bits!

Recognising the gaps between promised and actual performance and understanding why those variances occurred, that's a reactive process and simple research. Now you really have to earn your money.

What are you going to do to overcome any challenges and get us back on track to the Future State?

We have sat in thousands of strategy meetings and can assure you there is nothing more uncomfortable in business than being unable to propose a solution after presenting a problem. Expect long uncomfortable silences and searching stares. You *must* have an idea how to address the situation and a proposal ready to ensure you make the promised progress. It is not enough to rely on a lightbulb moment. What the situation demands is a brief thought-out written proposal on how you plan to get your hat back on track.

Business is fast changing and unpredictable. Progress is a series of short peaks and troughs, not a convenient straight line. How well you make adjustments to those events is how you guarantee performance in each business function.

Therefore, if you experience a sales deficit one month, rapidly adjust the expectations of the other 'hats' in the ring, because how quickly they re-adjust their own functions is critical to achieving profitability and realising your Future State.

One Hat at a Time

Keeping to the order of hats generates more purposeful action. It is that process that stress tests your big decisions.

As a result, you will be right more times than wrong.

First Hat:

- PAST: Is there a gap between promised and actual progress?

- PRESENT: Why? What did we learn?

- FUTURE: Now what are *you* going to do to make an improvement?

Then, in sequence, each functional 'Hat' is asked to answer the same series of questions.

LEADER → SALES → OPS → SUPPLY → PEOPLE → FINANCE

Responsibility for the respective business functions is not negotiable, you and you alone own your hat.

SCENE 3: Innovation

Up to this point, the process has been focused on the need to manage strategy effectively, to ensure the business is progressing as planned and to adjust quickly in the face of any new challenges. However, that is still not enough.

The Future Statement is not fixed in time, meaning that, when we can, we should accelerate our arrival date. You do that by outperforming the forecast.

To this end, all the functions, the hats, have a responsibility to be creative and boost performance with innovative ideas, in a bid to get ahead of plan. If you can arrive earlier at your destination, that benefits everyone, not least you as the entrepreneur, who will be able to live your ideal life in business sooner.

There are two types of innovation, planned and unplanned. Occasionally we recognise an opportunity for strategically important improvement in the day-to-day grind of business as usual. However, that's incidental, an accident. What is more likely to inject added power is to schedule regular stop and think moments.

Therefore, after *execution*, make time for *innovation*. Creativity is always on the agenda whenever you think about the Future State.

In the first two parts of the session, due diligence has been completed on your business performance.

You are then given the freedom to be 'crazy' again.

Unlike the structure needed in scenes 1 and 2 of the perfect meeting, scene 3 is intentionally without boundaries, meaning that each person 'wearing' a hat is given license to suggest new ideas for improvement in the other functions.

These proposals can be well researched or just the green shoots of an innovation, it really doesn't matter because the primary objective is to bring out new ideas, however outlandish, not to justify them. Then, at a future date, any proposals deemed worthy of further investigation are subjected to the usual scrutiny.

If a suggestion is considered an improvement on how we counter threats or create opportunities, then the proposer is tasked to research their idea and present a brief proposal at the next session.

WARNING: You're Unbalanced!

Directing the act of business is a play in three scenes:

1. FUTURE STATE – remember why
2. EXECUTION – the order of hats PAST PRESENT FUTURE
3. INNOVATION – no boundaries

We have never experienced a 'perfect meeting' when it comes to business direction.

Human beings don't fit nicely into boxes. It's not in our nature.

The goal of bringing 'order' to the proceedings is to enable *all* the voices responsible for directing a business to challenge and contribute in equal measure.

It is only by exploiting all the experience available to the full that you can make brilliant business decisions subjected to maximum scrutiny.

We fully accept that the role of business direction is challenging. On the one hand you must be unemotional and calculating. On the other hand you must be able to switch seamlessly to the crazy state, being creative and rejecting structure for innovation.

That is why there are three distinct phrases to the perfect meeting when it comes to making it happen; because when execution meets crazy, that creates avoidable risk and you fail to achieve your Future State.

Even when you adopt this approach, board thinking will still fail if the 'Hats' in the room are unbalanced.

This effect occurs when you have a dominant voice in a meeting (or in your own head, if solo). People have unique personalities, levels of confidence and communication styles. It is very easy for a discussion on direction to become unbalanced. In all likelihood you will not even realise this has happened.

This is an extremely dangerous state to be in as a business, because it means decisions remain relatively unchallenged. Opportunities and threats are missed.

It is the responsibility of the Chair (Leader hat) to ensure this never happens, to encourage less confident voices to speak out and challenge, to ensure louder voices do not dominate, and engender the confidence to direct.

Board thinking helps achieve a balance. However, as with all processes, it is only as effective as the people within it. A strong leader is vital to direct a business effectively.

Voices in Your Head

If you wear all the hats, or many, you need to know yourself intimately as a person. You must not shy away from the hats you are less experienced in, or let yourself subconsciously become a dominant voice in the functions you enjoy.

The chances of creating your Future State are intrinsically linked to your ability to exercise self-discipline.

If you inadvertently or intentionally neglect a function in the act of business, because you are out of your comfort zone or do not have the ability to perform that function effectively, the business suffers.

Once again, you must *know yourself*.

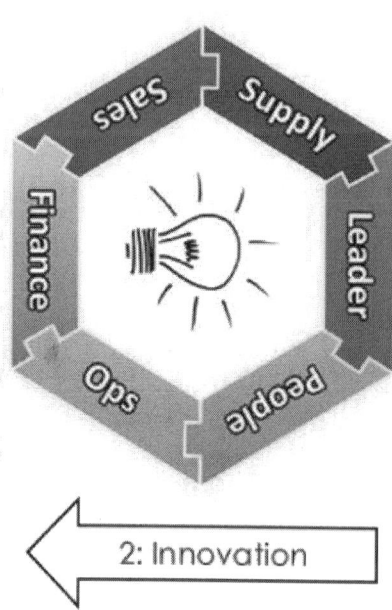

Agenda for "Board" Thinking

Tactical day to day is out. All about the bigger picture.

1: Execution

Future State

Any Other Business

Finance

People

Supply

Ops

Sales

Sales

Supply

Finance

Leader

Ops

People

2: Innovation

Chapter 15
Collaborate: Think Tank

We have now shared with you the Game Change ethos. The most powerful weapon in any business arsenal is always *you*.

We believe that the approach and techniques outlined in this book will enable you to have a focus and direction beyond anything you have experienced previously. However, we return to Dr Seuss for wisdom – "being crazy is not enough". We have outlined a structured process that will help you to stay on course to your Future State, while constantly injecting new energy into that journey. In addition, you now know how successful entrepreneurs operate and think. If you fail to realise your Future State it can be no one's fault but yours because you are the entrepreneur and business leader - you control your own destiny.

The decisions you make every day determine your level of success. Board thinking is a simple process to follow that ensures those choices are more likely to be fit for purpose. However, there is another level of scrutiny that the leading entrepreneurs commonly embrace – collaboration.

It is our firm belief that *every* entrepreneur should be collaborating with their peers - fellow business leaders.

Collaboration is *not* selling

The immediate response when we raise the idea of meeting fellow entrepreneurs on a regular basis is usually caution.

Everyone has had a bad experience going to a business breakfast or a networking lunch. We realise, of course, that business networking is an established and extremely popular tactical sales tool and accepted method of meeting new businesses. Groups like BNI and Chambers of Commerce are putting on these types of event all around the country every day. After attending these meetings many times in the past, we viewed traditional networking as simply another sales channel, one that didn't contribute to our own Future State. Therefore, at the start of our business, we decided it would be more effective to promote our brand where there wasn't a room full of competitors fighting for the same customers. It looked like a zero-sum game to us and we have never regretted the decision. However, as always you decide what is the best use of your valuable and finite time as an entrepreneur.

Before we can explain how business leader collaboration is fundamentally a different experience for an entrepreneur, we need to be very clear what it isn't.

It's *not* Tactical Networking

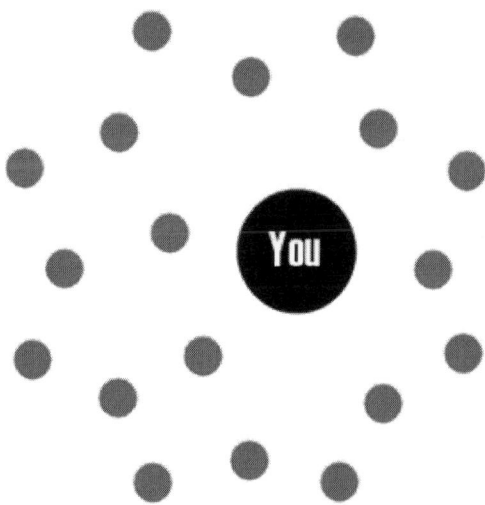

We have a lot of respect for people who enjoy (or put themselves through!) the traditional networking experience. It takes a special type of person to turn up at a business breakfast (or any event) and start working the room. Of course, the most effective networkers don't do that at all. They arrive having decided who to hunt down with an opening gambit and pitch fully prepared. Great networkers do nothing by accident.

For most of the entrepreneurs we have met, the general consensus is that these events generate little in terms of new business and are often nothing short of soul-destroying. That's partly the entrepreneur's fault for not arriving with their tactics ready and a clear objective.

Collaboration is *not* tactical networking because the underlying agenda for the latter process is business development, securing new sales. In addition, networking is random in nature, meaning you will encounter different people each time you attend. There is no guaranteed continuity.

That scenario might be acceptable when it comes to sales, but it is a huge barrier in terms of forming meaningful relationships which are based on trust. Even groups who insist on allowing only one of each trade to be a member are compromised when it comes to true collaboration because the primary motivation is still sales. We don't like the concept because the club mentality, passing each other work, clouds the integrity of a customer referral. You are also under intense peer pressure to introduce business within the group, which is never fun.

To bring balance to the argument, we have met people who attend these "closed shops" and say they do make a return on their investment of time and fees. If asked to join such a group, remember to ask why a free place has come available for that profession. There can only be two reasons, someone has moved away or it didn't deliver on the previous incumbent's investment and they left. Proceed with caution.

In our experience, the reason most entrepreneurs give for attending networking events is to break their feeling of isolation, which can be particularly intense and debilitating if you are a solo entrepreneur. In that respect, there is no doubt that a Danish pastry and swapping a few business stories can offer an emotional return on the investment. You may even exchange some business from time to time and secure some orders. However, we are talking about *transforming* your business future and that isn't going to do it, not unless you are extremely fortunate.

Far better to spend three hours seeking out strategically important named contacts and building relationships with them. In that scenario, there are no competitors looking over your shoulder, you have one-to-one time with the target and a chance to be remembered. Not surprisingly, we wholeheartedly buy into the concept of *strategic* networking.

Strategic Networking: The Power of Eight

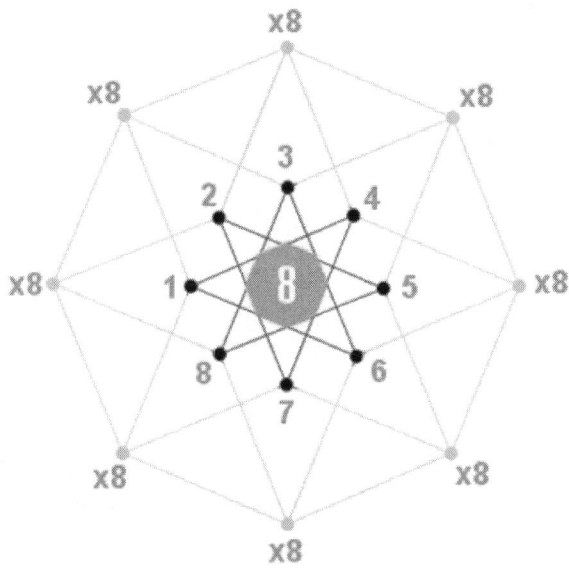

In 2001, I met the former PA to the Barclays Chief Executive (mentioned previously in the SIA: Money section). He shared a story on how Barclays became the leading banking organisation of the eighties and nineties. Every single person in that organisation was tasked to nurture and maintain a network of strategically important contacts relevant to their role. This process was not random or organic. The employees were asked to identify named individuals in organisations of their choice. Each person was encouraged to only have eight active relationships at any one time. This special octet consisted of the relationships that most merited an investment of time and effort because they could generate an exponential return in terms of sales. That didn't mean they refused to speak to anyone else. The eight relationships were not static and would evolve over time, as they ran their natural course and new ones were introduced.

We told this story to a room full of business leaders on a marketing programme a few years ago and, when we finished presenting, there was a deathly and uncharacteristic silence.

We asked whether anyone had an opinion and a woman in the audience said she disagreed entirely with the concept and that it made her extremely uncomfortable, describing it as "very eighties". She's right of course; it is unpalatable to consider managing your relationships with friends and acquaintances, but that's how successful organisations have been built for hundreds of years – developing strategically important alliances.

All Barclays had done was go a step further and codify the idea.

As a result, anyone in their organisation could understand and adopt the practice. Strategic networking executed correctly will have an exponential impact on your business, as each of your eight names has their own relationships to share.

You have to work hard on developing and maintaining special relationships, investing time and sometimes money (lunch!) into nurturing your network.

The *limit of eight* is based on the following assumptions:

- If more than eight, your relationships become contacts, which are less productive. It is not feasible to meaningfully nurture more than eight.

- If you have fewer than eight relationships, then you have time for more. You are missing opportunities.

The 'eight' is a nominal limit intended to bring some structure to the process. As we have pointed out repeatedly throughout this book, people are complicated and one size does not fit all.

The 'Power of Eight' approach helps you recognise which relationships are strategically important i.e., those that demand a constant investment of your time and energy.

We are definitely not advocating a 'Wall Street' type ruthless cull of the people you know!

However, we have no doubt whatsoever that there are eight people out there that you should be speaking to as an entrepreneur, named individuals who can accelerate and ease the journey to your Future State. Who are they? Contact them.

That is how simple the act of strategic networking can be.

But even this is still not true collaboration, as you still hold your own selfish agenda – increasing sales.

Business Think Tanks

Let us return for a moment to the whole purpose of collaborating with other entrepreneurs. It is to get different perspectives and experiences that can subject your decision making to a higher level of scrutiny. That means you make even more right decisions than wrong and your chances of realising your Future State are enhanced. Time is the most precious commodity for an entrepreneur because it is a finite resource. There is nothing you can do about that reality. As a business leader, you need to ensure that every hour of your time generates maximum return on investment. There will be no more valuable hour invested than attending an effective Think Tank and collaborating with your peers.

Bottom Up

We have spent twenty years working in the business support industry, observing the investment of billions of pounds by Government in supporting small and medium sized organisations, attempts to stimulate enterprise. Yet it is difficult to hide from the most stubborn statistic in business – a third of startups fail within three years (see Appendix B). That figure isn't only during this government, or even the previous one, but for the past thirty years.

While we are certain that a number of entrepreneurs benefited during those years, we have witnessed just two schemes that had a true legacy, meaning they continued beyond the period of investment provided by the funders of the scheme. These initiatives are the model for Think Tanks.

The first project was created and rolled out in Norfolk. The other project was launched in Devon, the other side of the country. Separated by hundreds of miles, none of the people involved in either group knew each other. They had never met before. Yet the model followed by both groups was identical.

These two groups of entrepreneurs continue to meet each month, almost a decade after launch. They do so because they greatly value the output from meeting fellow business leaders, so much so, that when funding was withdrawn, they decided to continue without the input of facilitators and Government support. These people took ownership of the format and made it their own. You will never have heard of these groups. They aren't part of a national branded scheme, the participants are simply ambitious entrepreneurs who meet to share their experiences and support each other. They are making it happen themselves, without any intervention from the government

Why on earth would they do this?

Why do businesses pay anything from £200 to £5000 a day to speak to a consultant? It's because they want new knowledge and perspectives based on a different experience. The power of a great consultant is not what they read in books and pass on, it's what they have experienced and can share.

Consultants meet many different businesses and bring alternative ways of thinking and working into your organization. They offer perspectives that are not forged in textbooks, but in the real world; they have *seen* what succeeded and failed.

You pay a consultant to save you the pain (money) of making similar mistakes. They improve the act of business by introducing new opportunities that may not have presented themselves previously. Or in other words you are paying to make better decisions. You shouldn't do that if you don't have to.

If the objective is to open your eyes to different ways of doing business, what could be more powerful than being part of a group of entrepreneurs and getting the information first hand, rather than through a third party?

That is the Think Tank model; a group of entrepreneurs that share their real life experience and challenge each other mercilessly on their business decisions, not because they get paid for an opinion but because they have an emotional stake in each other. They *care* what happens to each other's businesses because they know too well that those decisions can make or break their Future States; their lives.

The reason these two groups prosper ten years after their funding was pulled isn't because they were networking. It's too easy to assemble a room full of entrepreneurs and label that 'peer to peer learning'. The Government and private business support sector have been doing that for decades. To what end? Not much, if you judge the impact on reducing the business failure rate over a generation.

The alchemy at work in these two groups is the environment created to collaborate freely and without consequence. Those conditions were identical in both groups; despite being separated by hundreds of miles.

We will share with you these conditions because there is *no sterner* test on your decision making than peer to peer collaboration.

The Unwritten Contract

In our view, there are four primary drivers that stimulate people to collaborate:

1. Cups of Tea

A financial incentive transferred from one party to another. That may be as simple as tickets to a concert, but it is still a reward-based transaction.

In 2007, I attended one of my most challenging business meetings. For over an hour I struggled to see how an 80-year-old entrepreneur was generating sales. I am usually very quick to recognise the acts of business in organisations, but in this case nothing seemed to add up. After a while he stopped me in mid-sentence and said: "Elliot, it is cups of tea". On explanation it transpired that he would, literally, give cars to buyers who agreed to switch business to his company.

Now we don't recommend you do that (we were fairly sure it was illegal and made a hasty exit!). However, there is no starker example of a business relationship built on the shaky foundations of reward. When money changes hands that cannot be collaboration, as it's a one-way transaction. In this particular case, it was also a route to a million-pound turnover in less than two years. That's an uncomfortable truth for anyone competing in business.

2. New Ideas

New perspectives are a common and extremely positive driver for collaborative working. Each person is seeking new ideas on how to do business. An attendee at one of the two groups told us that he valued all opinions, even if he didn't agree with them. His view was that consultants tell you the right way, but there are thousands of entrepreneurs who achieve results using a different set of values, for example, following the 'wrong' way and being aggressively autocratic. He didn't agree with that approach, but hearing that perspective still made him think.

As a result, alternative experiences are shared between the parties and each entrepreneur makes more informed decisions. As P.T. Barnum said: "Four eyes see more than two". Exchanging new ideas is an equal transaction that works best when both parties share freely.

3. Love Seekers

Being a business leader can be an extremely isolating and stressful existence. Another positive driver of collaborative working is to exchange support and empathy, between people in the same boat as you. Collaborating with other entrepreneurs can inject a regular burst of positivity and light into your business life. Emotional capital is a powerful booster to enterprise. Many consultants make a good living just by listening to an entrepreneur's worries and concerns, sharing in both their successes and failures. It's called mentoring - a fixed and regular date in the diary to inject positivity and confidence. As we have pointed out repeatedly in this book, there are no more vital ingredients to being a great entrepreneur.

4. Altruism

Some people expect nothing in return for their collaboration. The act of sharing in itself is their return on investment. They share their experiences and support others only because they care. That process itself makes them happy, naturally boosting their positivity. If you are on the receiving end of this type of collaboration, it may feel like a one-way transaction, but your act of accepting support *is* their payback.

Common to all the drivers of collaboration is the absence of a written contract. True collaborative working is founded on an unsaid agreement, a psychological contract that lives only as long as all parties continue to agree to exchange value.

In summary, the advantages of collaboration are:

- Regular supply of new and alternative perspectives.
- Big decisions tested against real first-hand experience
- Avoidance of costly mistakes.
- Increased innovation, as a constant supply of new ideas.
- Emotional support for life as a leader.
- Isolation reduced - share success, share failure.
- Regular dose of inspiration – you inspire, but who inspires you?
- An opportunity to share and help others.

Whatever your initial driver may be for investing time in collaboration, once you enter into the process you receive all the benefits.

Creating the Collaborative Environment

Those two collaborative groups still flourish and survive to this day. They have not done so by accident. They collaborate effectively and share peer to peer experience because they buy into and follow a strict set of rules. Again, these are not prescriptive. They have evolved from a mutual understanding set out at the formation of their group. Or in other words, the constitution agreed upon before beginning their journey together.

The constitution at the heart of these two groups is virtually identical.

It may seem counter-intuitive to say you need to follow rules to be creative. However, that is precisely what makes these groups productive. The impact of peer to peer learning increases in direct relation to how much the participants trust each other.

If the value generated is insufficient, the group breaks up. That means signing up to a common code.

<u>Strictly NO Sales Agenda</u>

When you have a sales agenda and that is your primary driver for attending, then the openness needed to collaborate effectively is compromised. If you are trying to create new sales, go to a business breakfast, not a peer to peer group.

The Business Think Tank is bigger than that, it's a collaboration founded on sharing and mutual support. You might generate new business through the relationships in the group but that is *not* why you attend; that's a bonus benefit.

You never try to sell during a Think Tank session. In that sense, the agenda is the polar opposite of traditional networking.

<u>Absolute Trust</u>

In terms of testing business decisions to the full, that act is only possible if you have *all* the facts, be they business or life orientated.

Sharing personal information and hard earned experience is a significant challenge for any business leader because it is inherently risky. In business terms you are sharing knowledge that you paid for in terms of stress and money, competitive advantage that other people could use against you.

Sharing personal life details can be even more frightening, as you risk ridicule, appearing weak and vulnerable.

There's a time and a place for maintaining the illusion of great business performance. The Think Tank isn't it.

Trust between people in a collaborative support group must be explicit. When launching new groups, we always insist that the trust commitment to each other is not only acknowledged by each person, but that their promise exceeds the traditional standards in business.

The current accepted benchmark on trust is the Chatham House rules:

"When a meeting, or part thereof, is held under the Chatham House Rule, participants are free to use the information received, but neither the identity nor the affiliation of the speaker(s), nor that of any other participant, may be revealed."

Source: www.chathamhouse.org September, 2015

That's not good enough.

In a Think Tank nothing *ever* leaves the room. That's the level of commitment needed to foster true collaborative working.

<u>Group Led</u>

Everyone is equal in a Think Tank because each person had the guts and initiative to start up in business.

The number of people you employ, or the level of turnover you have achieved, should hold no weight in a collaborative working environment. After all, it is different perspectives that add the most value when we test our business decisions. Start-up entrepreneurs have insight to offer the leaders of large businesses and vice versa.

While a Chair is needed to ensure the collaborative session takes place in the first place, their style must be light and a short agenda should be used. This deliberate lack of structure allows the participants to dictate the direction of discussions and be creative.

Time is the only managed element, ensuring all the participants have ample opportunity to ask for help. For once, a strong external facilitator is a negative because the power of collaboration is boosted by lack of structure and freedom to think, not control.

That's an uncomfortable idea for most business support professionals and anyone in government, because you can't predict or measure the output. However, that is the point; the group leads.

Non-Competing

At the risk of stating the obvious, for effective collaboration you cannot be in the same market as someone else in the group.

"Some people have a foolish habit of telling their business secrets. If they make money they like to tell their neighbours how it was done. Nothing is gained by this, and oft times much is lost."

Source: The Golden Rules of Money Making. P.T. Barnum (1880).

The Think Tank approach is contrary to accepted opinion on peer to peer working, which is to cluster similar businesses within the same sector. The thinking behind that approach is that entrepreneurs will share the unique challenges of their industry. That's wishful thinking!

Firstly, only a fool tells the competition how they manage to win customers.

Secondly, after twenty years, we have worked in almost every sector and can assure you that the act of business is the same in all of them, regardless of the flavour. There are no significant differences. Believe your sector is extra special if you want, but that will close your mind to other ways of doing business, ones your competitors don't know about.

Thirdly, same sector collaboration is never going to achieve the higher level of trust needed to foster perfect collaborative working. The level of *difference* in experience determines the value added.

These are the primary reasons behind the longevity of these two groups – the participants are non-competing.

In terms of traditional networking, there is a logic to assembling businesses in the same sector (the supply chain) but to achieve true peer to peer collaboration, these 'same sector' groups are highly unlikely to work.

To collaborate, you need to share your business secrets to get accurate scrutiny on your decisions.

If you surround yourself with clones of your own business, then you effectively surround yourself with echoes - the level of challenge is diluted.

In the two groups, the entrepreneurs all operate in *different* markets.

<u>One Challenge at a Time</u>

Through discipline and respect, each person is given the time to explain their business challenge.

Free for all debate is not conducive to effective collaborative working.

Each participant in the group must be given an opportunity to provide their own individual experience and perspective on how to overcome an issue.

The discipline to focus on one challenge at a time in a discussion ensures everybody contributes and that thinking is subjected to maximum scrutiny.

That means you make better decisions.

<u>Continuity</u>

Another difference between a Think Tank and the traditional peer to peer approach is the closed door policy.

As we have said previously, the level of trust influences how much value you can generate from collaboration. If you are constantly seeing new faces at your sessions, you remain in a constant state of flux when it comes to trust.

In the original two groups, and those we have launched since, there is continuity. Groups maintain a bank of 10 to 20 entrepreneurs, with an average of two thirds in attendance at any face-to-face meetings. The level of people turnover is extremely low.

Over a ten-year period these entrepreneurs have developed unconditional trust because they got to *know each other personally*.

There is natural succession as entrepreneurs choose to move on or retire, but that is the only reason new faces are introduced.

Better to have explicit trust with a few experienced peers than superficial trust with many. These entrepreneurs have become business friends. Not in a meaningless marketing way, but intimately, because together they shared the highs and lows of their lives in business.

KEEP IT SIMPLE TO SUCCEED

Don't wait for someone else to set up a Think Tank. Call up two business people you respect and ask them to form the group with you. Ask them to introduce a contact each, and so on until you have a group of twelve entrepreneurs in non-competing sectors. The Agenda for your first meeting is simply to meet, have a drink and introduce yourselves. As a group, agree your *own* constitution. You must make it your own, as one size does not fit all. However, we share with you below the short list of conditions that have proven to underpin an effective collaborative working environment.

1. Strictly NO Sales Agenda.
2. Absolute Trust – nothing leaves the room.
3. Group Led.
4. Non-Competing.
5. One Challenge at a Time – discipline and respect.
6. Continuity – the group is invitation only.

The Challenge for a Second Meeting is *"Bring a Problem to Work Day"*. Use a simple agenda every time:

- Update on progress made on issues since last session.
- Round table presentation of challenges, inviting group input.
- Free discussion.
- A drink at the bar.

You just created your own FREE peer to peer consultancy. That's it then. We're off to the Job Centre!

Remember, you breathe the same air as every other entrepreneur in history. Be intimidated by *no one*. Respect *everyone*.

Game change your business. Game change your *life*.

Chapter 16
Game Change

Keep it simple to succeed is far from a new concept in business. However, we did not learn what 'simple' is from a book or training course. Instead, we have shared with you the best approach, strategies and tactics that we have *seen and experienced* over the past twenty years.

The Game Change book is intentionally short. Our goal was for anyone thinking of starting a business, or wanting to grow their existing enterprise, to read the book in a single session, close it, and think: "I can do that".

As active members of the business consultancy sector, it would be impossible for us to finish this book without making a comment on the current state of support for entrepreneurs, particularly the help available for young people starting their first business after completing their studies.

In 2011, Business Think interviewed the leading Conservative and former Deputy Prime Minister Lord Heseltine for our first book, 'Intervention'.

We challenged him about the lack of direction evident in businesses and why no one had ever tried to tackle this issue.

As you now know, we believe this is the primary barrier to overcoming the seemingly immovable business failure rate.

A transcript from that interview follows.

EF: Elliot Forte, Business Think
LH: Lord Heseltine

EF   "I have worked with approximately two thousand small and medium sized businesses. What strikes me that whole time is that Business Link policy was always about management improvement. In every company I met it wasn't about management, it was about the leader's capability to be entrepreneurial. So I would go into a company and talk about management, but actually it was more about scope to be enterprising.

I just wondered why that was, or even if that was the case?"

LH   "I'm not sure I know how you distinguish between the two."

That wasn't very encouraging. How can you address a problem if the people in charge don't even acknowledge it exists? However, having met the man, we don't believe for one second that a politician and entrepreneur with the experience of Lord Heseltine doesn't think there is a huge difference between management and direction.

So why the resistance?

The interview continued and we pressed the point.

EF   "Of a thousand companies that I personally worked with, I would estimate one in thirty hold any strategy meetings at all, one in two hundred have a non-executive Director of any kind and, while I am being cynical, that is often an accountant who'd done them a favour or a friend. Not what I imagine the role to be.

One in a thousand would actually be thinking like a Board or using Institute of Directors' principles. My conclusion is this. In small business we have a nation of managers not Directors at Board level. Why did Government not target this issue?"

LH   "Well. On that you would have two schools of thought. You would have the left wing, who wouldn't have any real interest in effective management of the capitalist system and you would have a very powerful element on the right wing of politics that would think it's a matter for the capitalist system to manage itself and government intervention, as they would call it, would be very unattractive, unlikely to achieve anything and bureaucratic.

So you have a much polarised approach to the sort of issues you're asking me about. I don't share that approach. But the climate here would be very hostile to it, including the climate of organisations that claim to represent small businesses."

EF   "Why would that be? I mean it's the top of the tree isn't it? A significant percentage of people at the top are lacking an understanding to effectively govern or direct small businesses. So everything below must not be as good as it could be."

LH   "Because the business climate of either overbearing intervention which comes from the left, or non-intervention which comes from the right. That's two much polarised positions, which I don't share.

My Party would not take kindly to the arguments that you should have these in-depth support systems.

I'm also deeply aware that there is a very substantial body of opinion, which would reflect itself in many of the representative organisations and in many of the newspapers, the populist newspapers I should say, which would be very suspicious of anything that smacked of interventionism. Or industrial strategy, another non-word, a non-idea.

But I believe in industrial strategy."

Lord Heseltine's statement explains why there has never been any action on the issue of direction under Government industrial policy.

It's not because the powers that be think it won't have an impact on the business failure rate.

Rather it is due to their personal ideological entrenchment.

As we have stated repeatedly in this book, if you keep doing the same thing you will keep getting the same result. To 'game change' a situation requires doing something different, implementing a new direction and strategy. That equation is true in most aspects of life and most definitely applies in both business and politics.

But endless intervention in business is not the answer. That approach tackles the symptoms, not the cause. Reduce dependency early by removing a need for corrective business support.

Traditional teaching of business studies, economics and management (including MBAs), is not preparing people for the real challenge in business, the positive and negative emotions that attack the senses in enterprise. These are the barriers to maintaining an entrepreneurial mind. The evidence is there for all to see. If the traditional approach worked, this country wouldn't have had such a shameful and stubborn business failure rate for a generation.

If you keep doing the same thing, you'll keep getting the same result. If you have ever started a business, you know this already. The most serious barriers to success are those of a personal nature, not commercial.

We have worked at the coalface with thousands of businesses and observed that pain first hand. We have witnessed husband and wife teams whose marriages failed due to the stress of running a small business. We have worked with family businesses where the rules of business are torn up and the potential for emotional conflict constantly simmers just below the surface. We have worked with entrepreneurs who have died in the middle of projects. These are the real threats that end organisations and ruin lives.

Life changing events *brought on* by the pressure of business.

Until young people, the business leaders of the future, understand the excitement of enterprise and are properly prepared to deal with its emotional challenges, the need for intervention (and consultancy) will never subside. Thinking like a Board and business direction are critical skills that equip entrepreneurs to avoid pitfalls.

At the moment, every young entrepreneur steps onto the learning curve at the lowest point and experiences the shock of first time business. This is an experience that some will survive and grow, others will survive but flounder and a few will not survive at all.

As business leaders we must all share the responsibility to better prepare our young people for a life in business. That is why altering the current status quo must be bottom up. To that end we have given you our insight, experience and knowledge on the Think Tanks model. We do so willingly and ask for no reward. Any author commissions from sales of the Game Change book will be donated to The Prince's Trust, a youth charity that helps young people aged 13 to 30 get into enterprise, jobs and education.

Because our vision at Business Think is for every entrepreneur to be regularly collaborating, sharing experience, challenging each other and receiving the critical emotional support we all need in business. On that day the need for remedial and corrective consultancy will be redundant.

So our challenge to you is this:

Form a Think Tank.
PUT US OUT OF WORK.

Appendix A:
Start Up Email

Full and unedited transcript of email sent to Elliot Forte by James Forte on 19th August 2000.

"You have done the right thing for sure. It must be in Nana's genes as Gramp always said 'you didn't get it from me'. Believe me it isn't hard. There are 365 days in a year to make money in, so don't panic if nothing happens at first and don't ever get despondent.

If you are not enjoying it, or feel tired, or you are having a bad day ... leave everything for an hour or so, and have a rest. Everybody's lowest time of despair is in the early hours of the morning, you wake up and literally feel sick with worry.

You will master this when you realise that nobody can fire you, and you cannot be shot either, whatever you do.

You are answerable to absolutely nobody. They can take your company, they can take your house, and they can take all your possessions as well. They cannot take your wife, your children, your family, your friends, your pride or your ability to start again. They never had the balls to do it themselves so treat them with the contempt they deserve.

Humour people as you take money from them.

The #1 rule of business is if you give someone a pound, and they give you a pound and a penny ... then you are in front.

The #2 rule is knowing when you are losing money.

The #3 rule is not repeating the same mistake that caused the loss.

Good luck and if there is anything I can do for you, then call. I mean it."

Appendix B:
UK Business Survival Rates

Decline in the 3 Year Survival Rate Since 1995

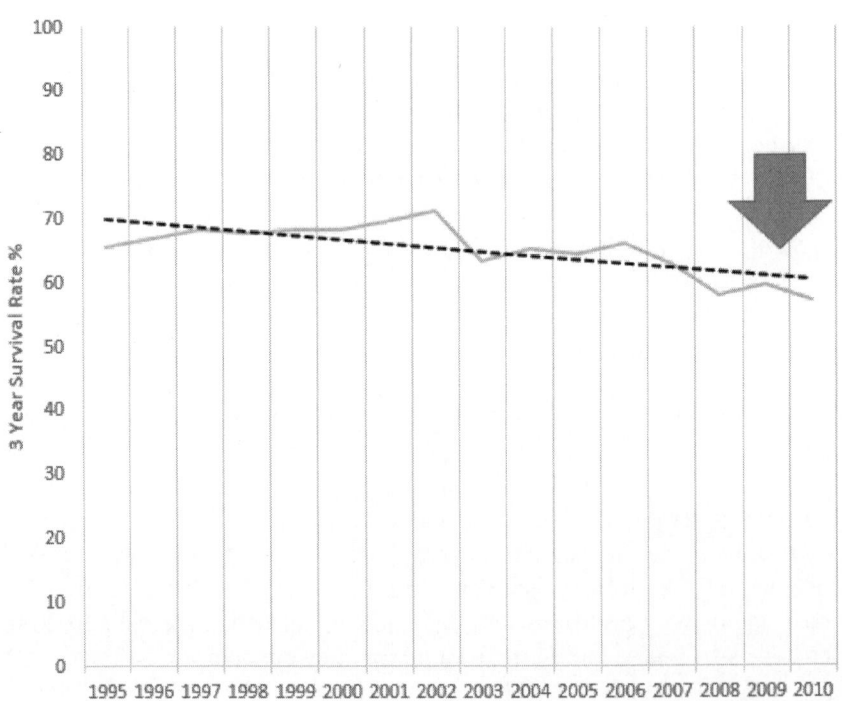

Since 2004, on average, 38.0% of start-ups *failed* to survive 3 trading years.

Year Started	2010	2009	2008	2007	2006	2005	2004	2003
3 Year Survival %	57.1	59.6	58	63	66.2	64.7	65.3	63.6

Year Started	2002	2001	2000	1999	1998	1997	1996	1995
3 Year Survival %	71.3	69.7	68.4	68.3	67.7	68.5	66.9	65.6

Decline in the 5 Year Survival Rate Since 2004

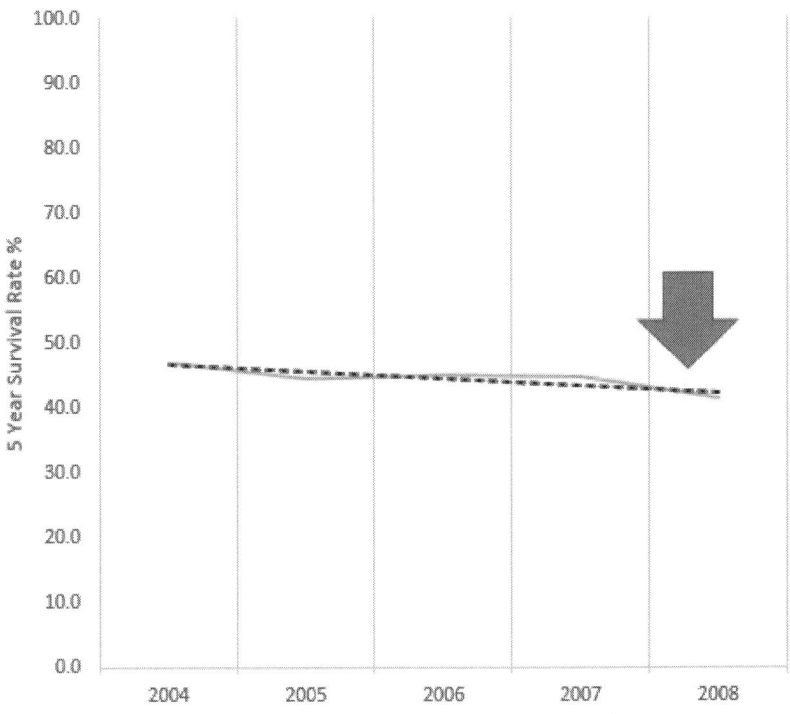

Since 2004, on average, 55.6% of start-ups *failed* to survive 5 trading years.

Year Started	2008	2007	2006	2005	2004
5 Year Survival %	41.3	44.6	45.0	44.4	46.8

N.B. Records on 5-year survival rates have been published since 2004. The next update from the Office of National Statistics will be published November 2015.

Source:
Business Demography 2013. Released 27/11/14 by Office for National Statistics
SBS SME Statistics Business Survival Rates - 19 February 2007

Appendix C: Future State Examples

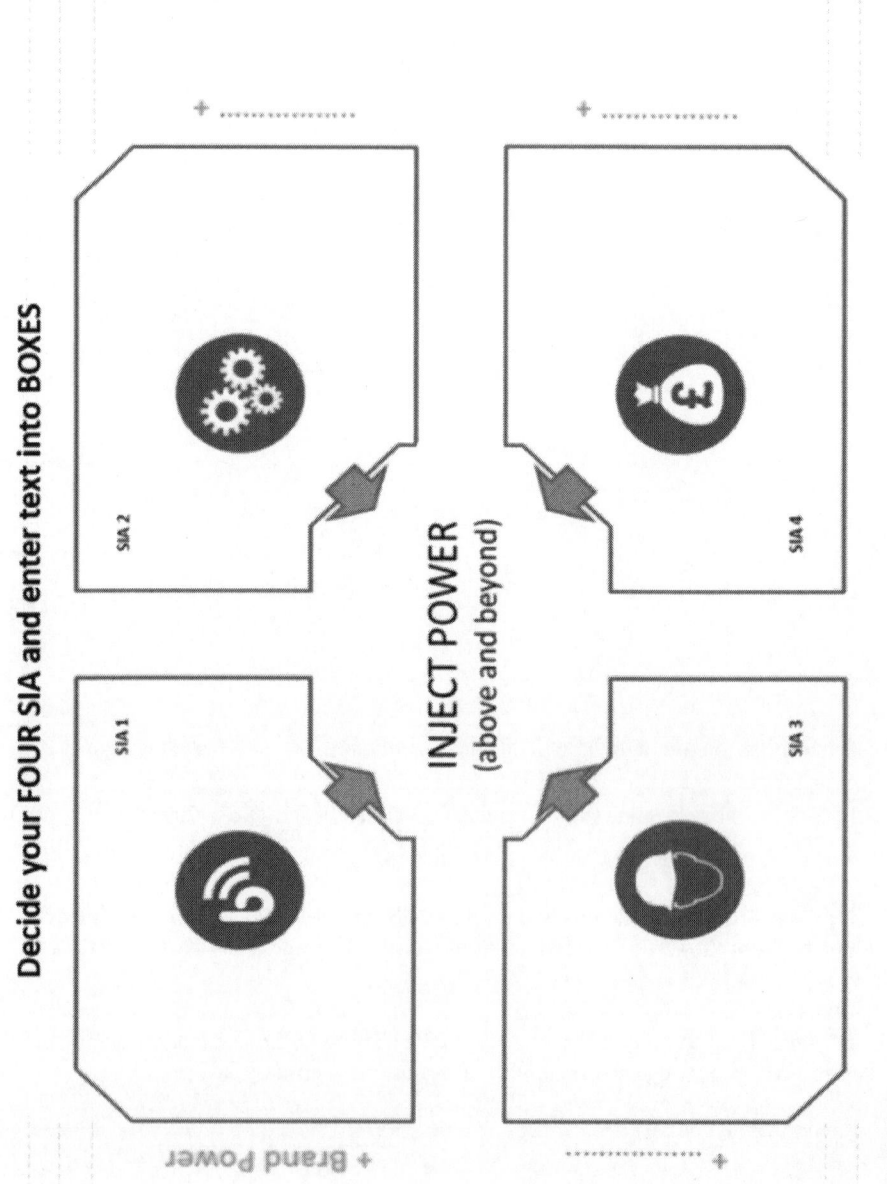

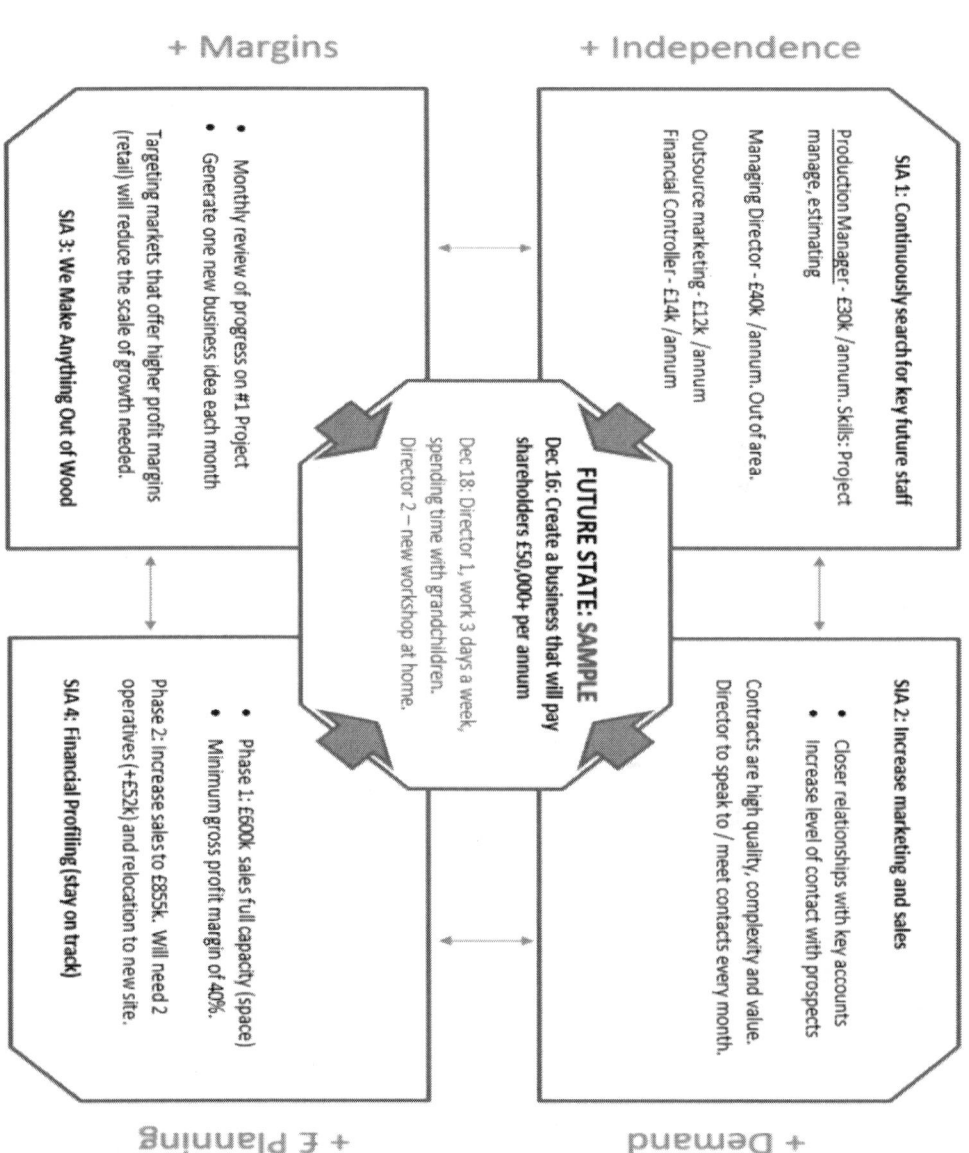

+ Margins

+ Independence

+ £ Planning

+ Demand

FUTURE STATE: SAMPLE

Dec 16: Create a business that will pay shareholders £50,000+ per annum

Dec 18: Director 1, work 3 days a week, spending time with grandchildren. Director 2 – new workshop at home.

SIA 1: Continuously search for key future staff

Production Manager - £30k /annum. Skills: Project manage, estimating

Managing Director - £40k /annum. Out of area.

Outsource marketing - £12k /annum

Financial Controller - £14k /annum

SIA 2: Increase marketing and sales

- Closer relationships with key accounts
- Increase level of contact with prospects

Contracts are high quality, complexity and value. Director to speak to / meet contacts every month.

SIA 3: We Make Anything Out of Wood

- Monthly review of progress on #1 Project
- Generate one new business idea each month

Targeting markets that offer higher profit margins (retail) will reduce the scale of growth needed.

SIA 4: Financial Profiling (stay on track)

- Phase 1: £600k sales full capacity (space)
- Minimum gross profit margin of 40%.

Phase 2: Increase sales to £855k. Will need 2 operatives (+£52k) and relocation to new site.

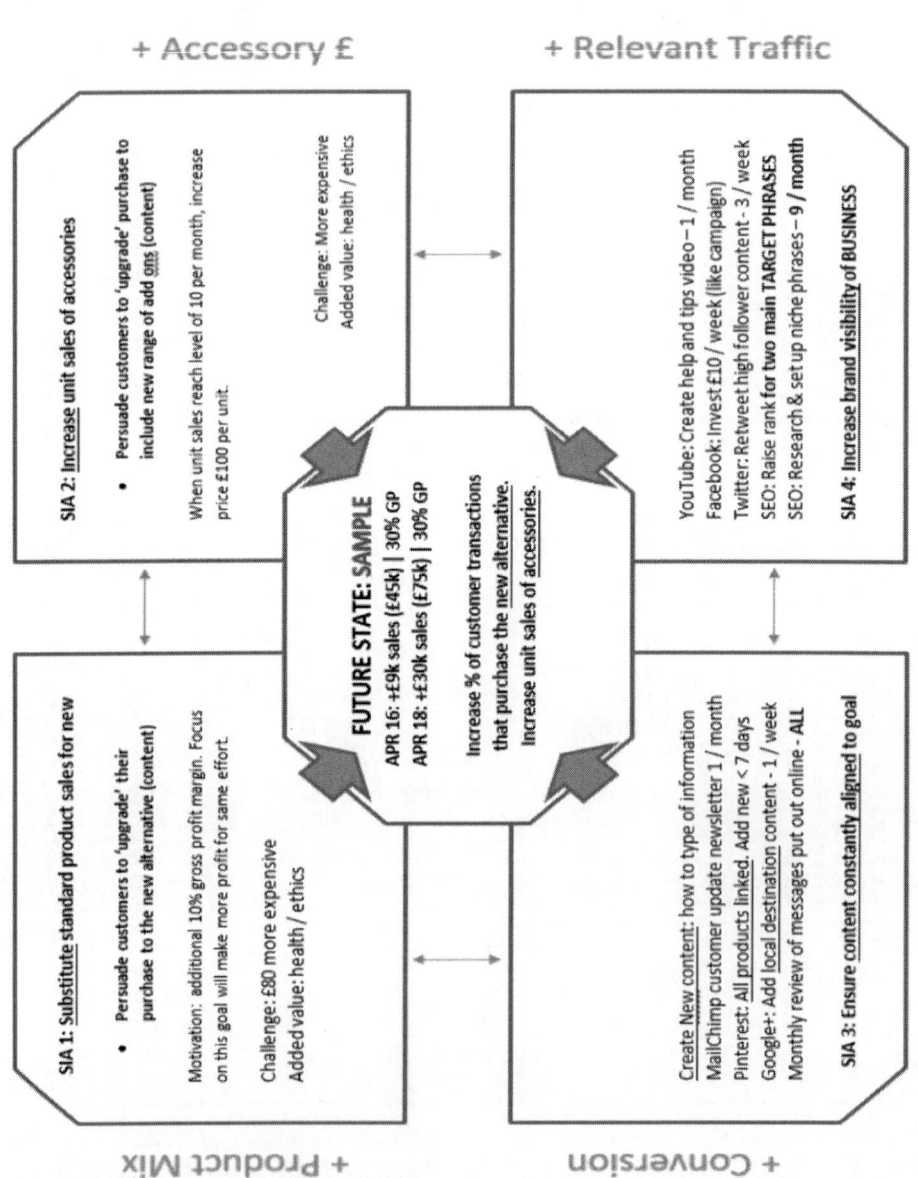

+ Accessory £

+ Relevant Traffic

SIA 2: Increase unit sales of accessories

- Persuade customers to 'upgrade' purchase to include new range of add ons (content)

When unit sales reach level of 10 per month, increase price £100 per unit.

Challenge: More expensive
Added value: health / ethics

YouTube: Create help and tips video – 1 / month
Facebook: Invest £10 / week (like campaign)
Twitter: Retweet high follower content – 3 / week
SEO: Raise rank for two main TARGET PHRASES
SEO: Research & set up niche phrases – 9 / month

SIA 4: Increase brand visibility of BUSINESS

FUTURE STATE: SAMPLE

APR 16: +£9k sales (£45k) | 30% GP
APR 18: +£30k sales (£75k) | 30% GP

Increase % of customer transactions that purchase the new alternative.
Increase unit sales of accessories.

SIA 1: Substitute standard product sales for new

- Persuade customers to 'upgrade' their purchase to the new alternative (content)

Motivation: additional 10% gross profit margin. Focus on this goal will make more profit for same effort.

Challenge: £80 more expensive
Added value: health / ethics

Create New content: how to type of information
MailChimp customer update newsletter 1 / month
Pinterest: All products linked. Add new < 7 days
Google+: Add local destination content - 1 / week
Monthly review of messages put out online - ALL

SIA 3: Ensure content constantly aligned to goal

+ Product Mix

+ Conversion

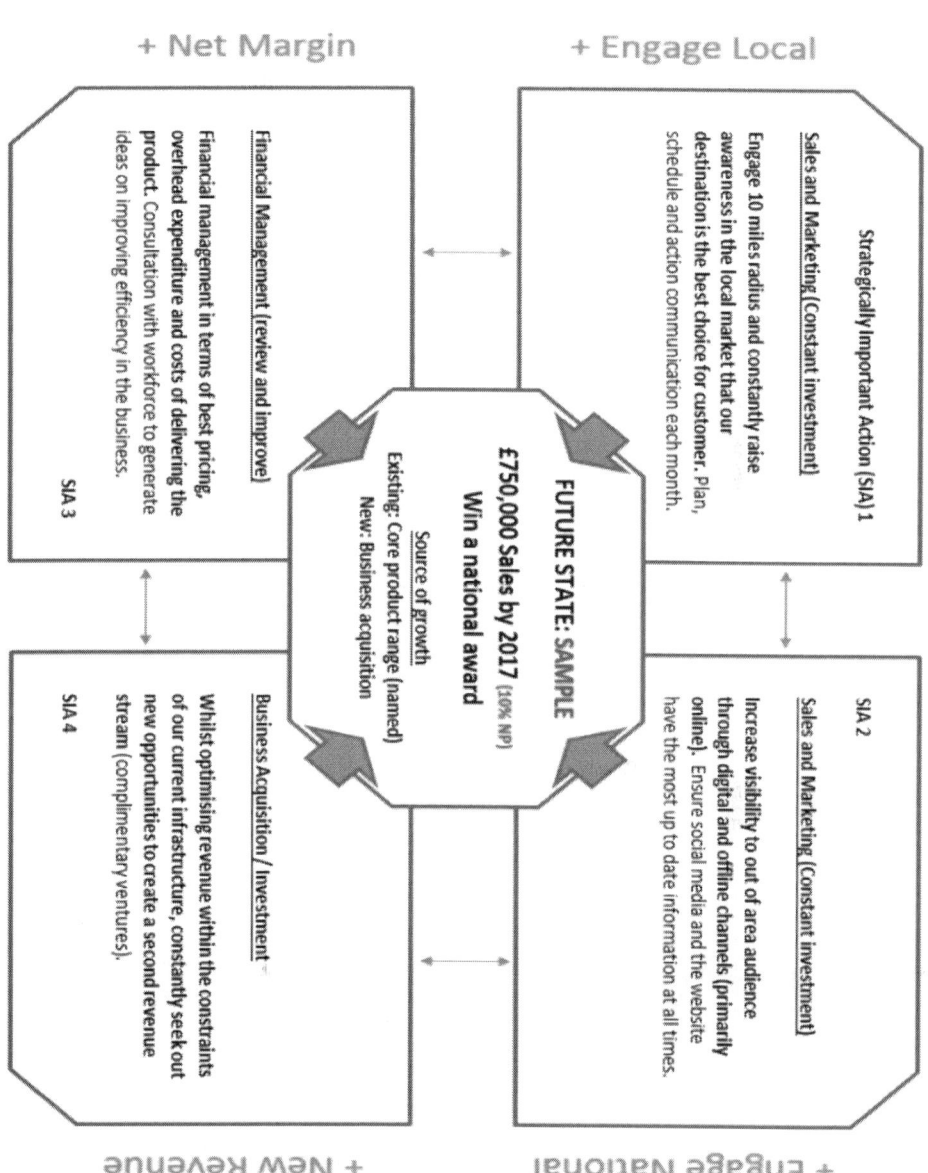

Strategically Important Action (SIA) 1

Sales and Marketing (Constant investment)

Engage 10 miles radius and constantly raise awareness in the local market that our destination is the best choice for customer. Plan, schedule and action communication each month.

Financial Management (review and improve)

Financial management in terms of best pricing, overhead expenditure and costs of delivering the product. Consultation with workforce to generate ideas on improving efficiency in the business.

SIA 3

FUTURE STATE: SAMPLE

£750,000 Sales by 2017 (10% NP)
Win a national award

Source of growth
Existing: Core product range (named)
New: Business acquisition

SIA 2

Sales and Marketing (Constant investment)

Increase visibility to out of area audience through digital and offline channels (primarily online). Ensure social media and the website have the most up to date information at all times.

Business Acquisition / Investment

Whilst optimising revenue within the constraints of our current infrastructure, constantly seek out new opportunities to create a second revenue stream (complimentary ventures).

SIA 4

SIA 2

Constantly communicate with 50 miles radius to raise brand awareness and reputation.

Invest in marketing material that represents the brand values of the company and why customers would use us ahead of any other supplier.

Constantly seek out new efficiencies and time savings by examining what we DO in terms of sales, buying, fulfilment and finance.

Releasing repetitive activity will release more time for high impact activity (sales, brand, Africa etc.)

SIA 4

FUTURE STATE: SAMPLE

£1 million sales by end 2016

Source of growth
UK: Core Product Range
Asia and Africa: Green products
Existing / New Customers

Strategically Important Action (SIA) 1

Constantly invest in developing a brand renowned for being technically expert and able to provide cost effective solutions to complex and challenging pump scenarios.

Enhance this perception by investing in the highest levels of customer service.

Constantly invest 20% of business development time in expanding Africa market, identifying new contacts, nurturing these relationships and MEETING potential distributors in these countries.

Lead responsibility: Director 1

SIA 3

Appendix D:
Game Change Workbook

Task 1: Write Your Future Statement

When writing your Future Statement, you need to be brief and succinct. Avoid being generic, be specific and not limiting but above all, it needs to be personal to you.

Three sentences – what is your ideal life, what does that equate to financially, and when do you want to be there (not how)?

Your Future Statement = Qualitative + Quantitative + Time-Based

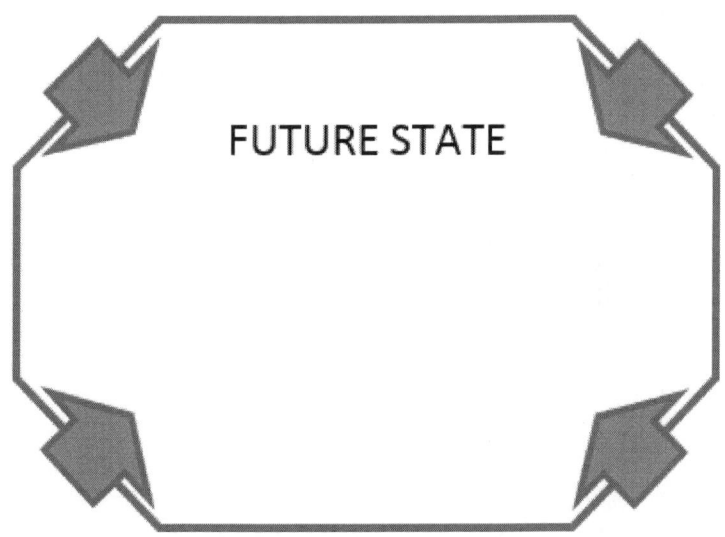

FUTURE STATE

If you can't make your Future State fit in this box, it's still too complicated. Need some help? See 'Appendix C' for real examples.

Task 2: The Business Life Cycle

Plot your monthly net profit from start up to current day. Is the trend upwards or downwards? Where do you think your organization is on the Business Life Cycle curve? Are you employing the right strategies?

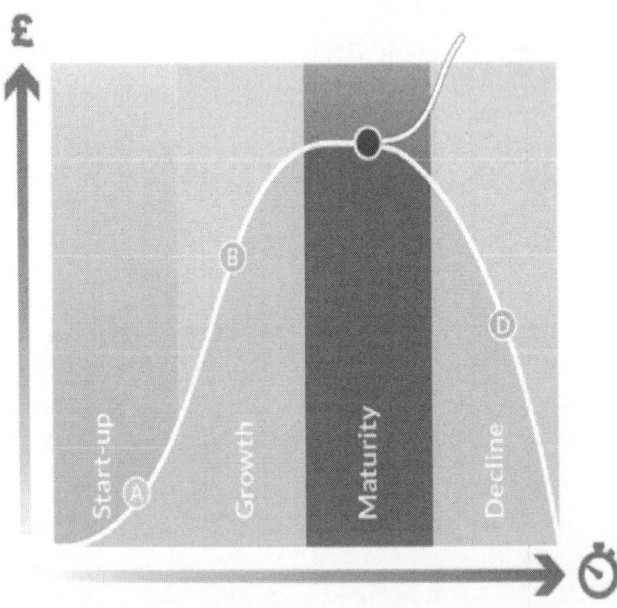

Start: Create Life	**Sales and marketing** to create demand.
A: Sustain Life	Must **deliver on promises** (brand) – **operations**.
B: Payback	**Finance** pace of growth (don't run out of cash!).
C: Peaking	Competitors caught up. Innovate: **Create a new curve** (rebirth)!
D: Decline to Death	No time to innovate. Must rapidly **diversify** or plan for **exit**.

If it hasn't already, when do you think your business will reach the *Peaking* phase? Why? What can you do about it?

Task 3: Check Your Enterprise State

Please read the following 8 scenarios and answer the questions using the scale of 1 (never) to 10 (definitely)...

A: Thanks to your excellent sales and marketing you have a won a new contract. Your business can just about handle the new workload and it's a great opportunity for the business.

Would you subcontract this work to another business?

B: Your business is growing, but financing production has caused temporary cash flow issues. You are approached by a supplier letting you know a respectable competitor is up for sale at a fair price.

Do you take steps to try and purchase this company?

C: You are completing your annual price review. It's been a great year but a handful of customers have suggested these are hard times. Your competitors have put their prices down recently.

Would you put your prices up?

D: The business has been making the same product for years. Currently there aren't any complaints. Our employees seem happy and perform well. We are making money. You are contacted by a trainer.

Would you spend money on motivational training for all your staff?

E: You have a critical delivery deadline to hit for one of your main customers. It's slightly behind schedule though the team are working hard to make it happen.

Would you ignore the situation at this stage?

F: You are booked to present an important seminar to prospective customers. A colleague has asked to go in your place and they seem keen to impress.

Would you arrange for this person to attend in your place?

G: Business is right on track. Everything seems to be working and the income is pouring in. There are a few challenges on the horizon but nothing you can't handle. It's a really busy time for you.

Would you agree to meet a new business consultant?

H: Your business has grown to the point where it is today. You have recently been to a bank seminar advocating that every organisation must have a written business plan to succeed.

Would you agree that a written plan is a "must have"?

Plot your eight answers on the following spider diagram and join the dots.

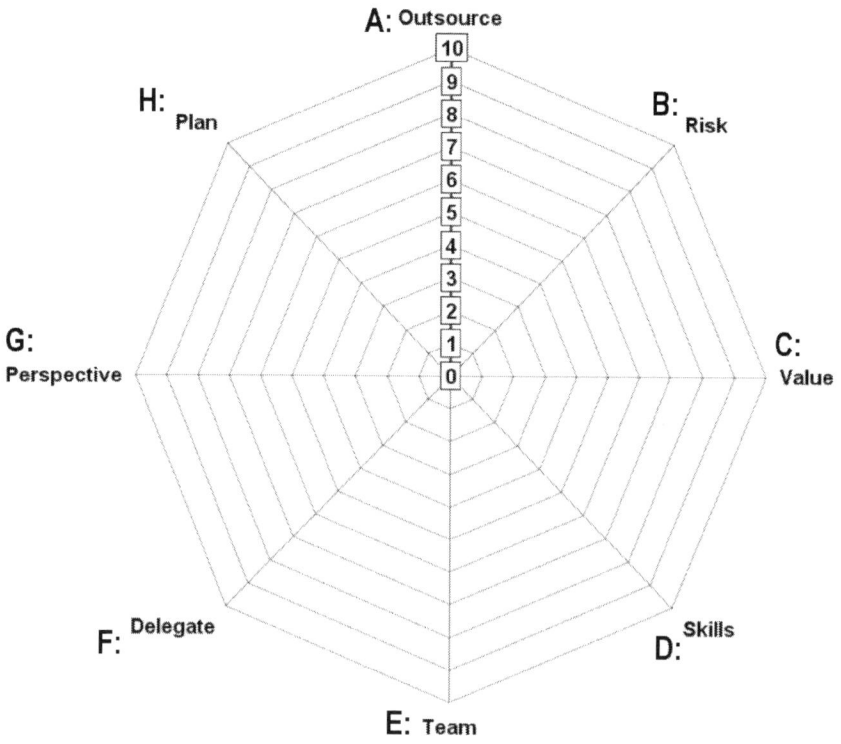

You are now looking at a visual representation of your enterprise state of mind at this precise moment. You KNOW YOURSELF.

Please note: this exercise is intended purely to embed the eight proverbs. There are no right or wrong answers!

To draw a perfect octagon (no one has ever scored all tens on the Game Change program) is a dangerous place to be as an entrepreneur. We all need at least a modicum of control!

Task 4: Capture Your Brand Promise

Write down:

a) The values that guide you in your life and in business.
b) The rules that govern the way you and your business will conduct yourselves.
c) What you are you prepared to do and what you aren't prepared to do.
d) What emotions will your customers experience? Will they feel happy? Secure? Educated?
e) What you do that is valuable to your customers; how you add value for them.

This list is the essence of your brand. In fact, it is your brand.

Be continuously and acutely aware:

- When it comes to integrity one size does not fit all - always do what's right for you.
- Live your values and avoid culture shock i.e. promising one thing and delivering another.
- Nurture people to adopt your brand values in a way that suits them, don't dictate.
- Never compromise your brand promise for profit - customers will see right through you in time.
- LOVE your brand (and business).

Task 5: Decide Your Four Marketing Strategies

Action 1:

EXISTING/NEW products (services) to EXISTING customers

a) Define who your high value customers are (targets)
b) Write down a list of sales messages
c) Schedule a diary of contact

Then make sure you have the resources in place to make it happen.

You must prioritise increasing existing customer spend over the other strategies in the matrix because this easier money helps fund the rest. Financing your campaigns and reaching your Future State will be far more challenging if you fail to do so.

Action 2:

Decide your four strategies (one for each box in the matrix on page 89). Ideas that will better engage new, existing and past customers.

1 SERVICE | 2 INFORM | 3 PROMOTE | 4 INNOVATE

N.B. Your ideas must be ABOVE and BEYOND what you already do in terms of marketing and sales. The ideas must contribute to accelerating your Future State.

Task 6: Improve Your Processes

a) Review your Future Statement and Above and Beyond Marketing.

b) Isolate a process that is critical to adding value for the target customers.

c) Observe and draw the steps in that process from start to finish (see Chapter 8).

d) Invite the people involved in the process to discuss the drawing and suggest revisions (based on their experience); that may be just you!

e) Classify each step as <u>V</u>alue Adding, <u>E</u>ssential or <u>N</u>on Value.

f) Estimate level of risk to profit margins at the interfaces.

g) Suggest improvements.

Your ideas must be ABOVE and BEYOND what you already do in terms of process improvement and must directly contribute to realising your Future State.

Task 7: Check Skills and Capacity Requirements

a) Review your Future State and Strategically Important Actions in Marketing and Sales, and Process.

b) What are the key worker roles needed to achieve your future state?

c) What skills and experience do these people need (capability)?

d) Are these people already working in the business?

e) If not, what are you going to do about it and when?

f) Devise a people review process that fits with the culture of your business and implement it

Your ideas must be ABOVE and BEYOND what you already do in terms of people improvement and must contribute to your Future State.

Task 8: Increase Profit Margins

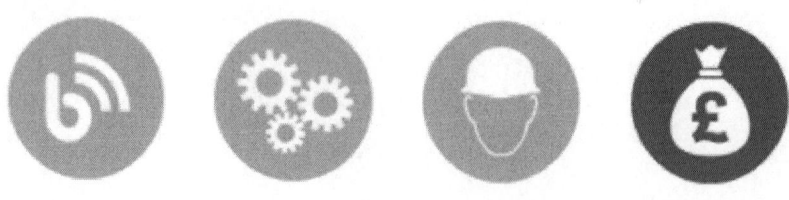

a) Review your Future State and Strategically Important Action in Marketing and Sales, Process and People needs.

b) What opportunities are there for raising prices?

c) What opportunities are there for achieving savings in the costs of doing and reducing costs of existence, without compromising value and brand?

d) What do you need to do?

e) When?

Your ideas must be ABOVE and BEYOND what you already do in terms of financial improvement and must directly contribute to realising your Future State.

Task 9: Fill in Your Future State

A copy of the blank Future State template can be downloaded online at www.gamechangebook.com.

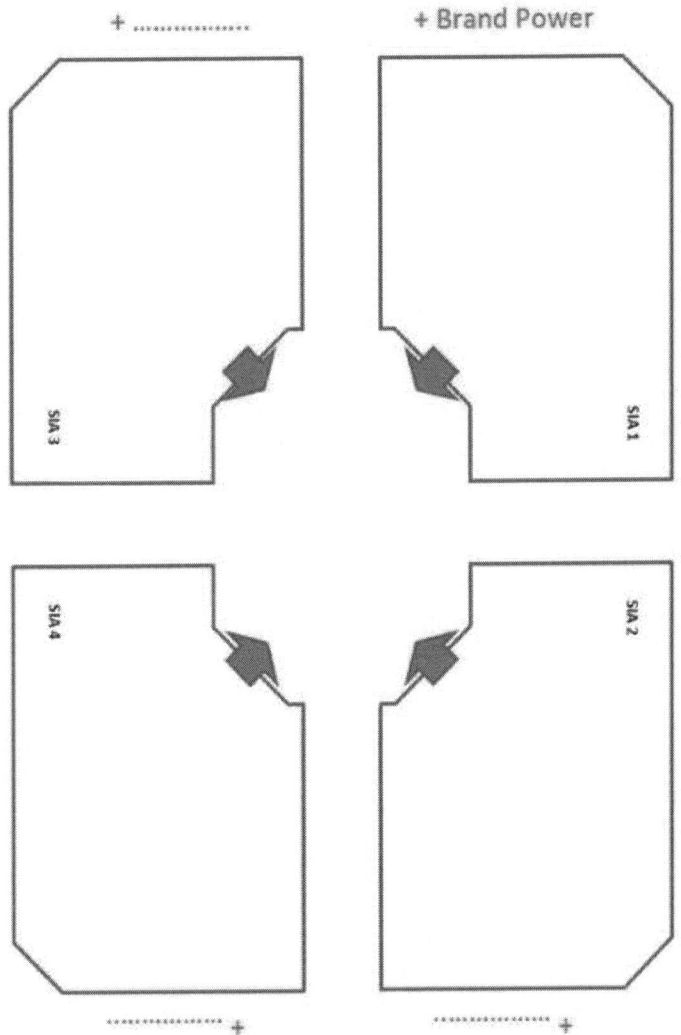

Task 10: Decide which *named individual* 'OWNS' each business hat.

We can all contribute, but someone must have lead responsibility.
NB. You might wear them all!

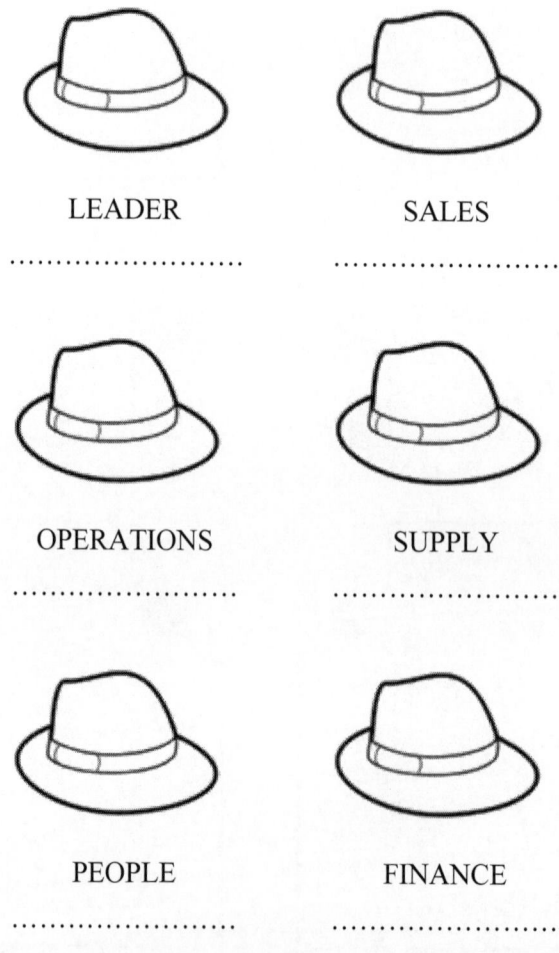

LEADER

....

SALES

....

OPERATIONS

....

SUPPLY

....

PEOPLE

....

FINANCE

....

Do you have, or do you need, a 'special' Hat?

1: Execution

Any Other Business

Future State

Agenda for "Board" Thinking

Tactical day to day is out. All about the bigger picture.

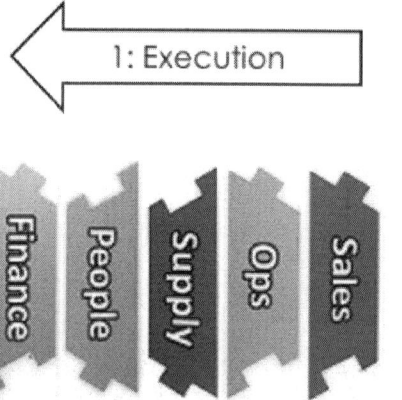

2: Innovation

Task 12: Form a Think Tank

Don't wait for someone else to set up a Think Tank. Call up two business people you respect and ask them to form the group with you. Ask them to introduce a contact each, and so on until you have a group of twelve entrepreneurs in non-competing sectors. The Agenda for your first meeting is simply to meet, have a drink and introduce yourselves. As a group, agree your *own* constitution. You must make it your own, as one size does not fit all. However, we share with you below the short list of conditions that have proven to underpin an effective collaborative working environment.

a) Strictly NO Sales Agenda.
b) Absolute Trust – nothing leaves the room.
c) Group Led.
d) Non-Competing.
e) One Challenge at a Time – discipline and respect.
f) Continuity – the group is invitation only.

The Challenge for a Second Meeting is *"Bring a Problem to Work Day"*.

Use a simple agenda every time:

- Update on progress made on issues since last session
- Round table presentation of challenges, inviting group input
- Free discussion
- A drink at the bar

Remember, you breathe the same air as every other entrepreneur in history. Be intimidated by *no one*. Respect *everyone*.

Game change your business.

Game change your *life*.

#0092 - 290416 - C0 - 210/148/12 - PB - DID1439566